WITH GOD
IN SOUTH SUDAN

OSCAR MOMANYI, SJ

WITH GOD
IN SOUTH SUDAN

OSCAR MOMANYI, SJ

MEREO
Cirencester

Mereo Books

1A The Wool Market Dyer Street Cirencester Gloucestershire GL7 2PR
An imprint of Memoirs Publishing www.mereobooks.com

WITH GOD IN SOUTH SUDAN

ISBN: 978-1-86151-870-5

First published in Great Britain in 2017
by Mereo Books, an imprint of Memoirs Publishing

Copyright ©2018

Oscar Momanyi, SJ has asserted his right under the Copyright Designs and Patents Act 1988 to be identified as the author of this work.

A CIP catalogue record for this book is available from the British Library.

This book is sold subject to the condition that it shall not by way of trade or otherwise be lent, resold, hired out or otherwise circulated without the publisher's prior consent in any form of binding or cover, other than that in which it is published and without a similar condition, including this condition being imposed on the subsequent purchaser.

The address for Memoirs Publishing Group Limited can be found at www.memoirspublishing.com

The Memoirs Publishing Group Ltd Reg. No. 7834348

The Memoirs Publishing Group supports both The Forest Stewardship Council® (FSC®) and the PEFC® leading international forest-certification organisations. Our books carrying both the FSC label and the PEFC® and are printed on FSC®-certified paper. FSC® is the only forest-certification scheme supported by the leading environmental organisations including Greenpeace. Our paper procurement policy can be found at www.memoirspublishing.com/environment

Typeset in 11/15pt Times New Roman
by Wiltshire Associates Publisher Services Ltd. Printed and bound in Great Britain by Printondemand-Worldwide, Peterborough PE2 6XD

For
Paul Besanceney, SJ
Norman Dickson, SJ
Bernard Mallia, SJ
Francis Njuguna, SJ (Deng Malual)
Salvador Ferrão, SJ
Herbert Liebl, SJ

For their courageous witness to the people
of Sudan and South Sudan

CONTENTS

	Preface	i
	Map of South Sudan	iii
	National Anthem of South Sudan	iv
1.	On the Threshold of Hope	1
2.	Entering Canaan	9
3.	Trusting in the Slow Work of God	27
4.	The Will to Help Others	50
5.	Taking One Day at a Time	67
6.	Things Fall Apart	82
7.	There and Back	93
8.	Going Further Still	102
9.	Making Old Things New	109
10.	Travelling Mercies	118
11.	Where God Weeps	129
12.	Giving a Lifetime?	150

PREFACE

This story is inspired by the experience I had in South Sudan. I was sent there to work at a time when the country was struggling to make a difficult transition. South Sudan got its independence from the Sudan on July 9, 2011. One year later, in July 2012, I found myself immersed in the post-independent South Sudan.

The Jesuits or the Society of Jesus, of which I am a member, is a worldwide missionary society established by Saint Ignatius of Loyola (1498-1556) in 1540. The Jesuits work in the most disadvantaged areas of the world. They are organized in regions known as provinces under the leadership of a superior. Some works which the Jesuits are involved in include spiritual ministries, accompanying refugees, and education. They are found in 112 countries in six continents. Pope Francis, the first Jesuit Pope, in his first exhortation as pope titled *Evangelii Gaudium* (*The Joy of the Gospel*), urged Christians and all people of good will not to forget the people living in the margins of society such as South Sudan.

As a member of the Society of Jesus, I was happy to be sent to work as a teacher at the Jesuit high school Loyola Secondary School in the town of Wau, South Sudan. South Sudan is a country that is struggling to get on its feet. It is not an easy place to venture into because of its troubled past, present crisis, and an uncertain future. The story that unfolds in the following pages is one of faith, hope, and love in the midst of uncertainty, the threat of war and violence.

What unfolds here is not a single story but rather an amalgam of stories. This book narrates my journeys, joys, challenges and the journeys and experiences of other people of faith as they accompanied the South Sudanese people. It is a story of a desire to be a witness to the values of the Gospel in a difficult situation.

In 1969, Pope Paul VI said the following while on a visit to

Uganda, "By now, you Africans are missionaries to yourselves. The Church of Christ is well and truly planted in this blessed soil." As an African, I had never thought of mission in this way. I thought that missionaries only came from Europe and America to work in Africa as I had observed in my native country Kenya. In the following pages, I will narrate some of the experiences I had when I responded to the call to be a missionary to my African people in South Sudan.

I would like to thank the following people who read earlier drafts of this work and made their valuable suggestions for improvement: Terry Hanley, Joy Kimemiah, Kathleen Shrader, Sr. Jane Ferdon, OP, Frs. Terry Charlton, SJ, Norman Dickson, SJ, and Augustine Ekeno, SJ. I am grateful to these friends for taking their time to check this work. However, I take responsibility for any errors that may be found in this narrative.

I would also like to thank Fr. Joseph Oduor Afulo, SJ the provincial superior of the Jesuits in Eastern African for approving this work for publication. Fr. John McGarry, SJ the superior of the Jesuit Community in Berkeley, CA requires a special thank you. He not only read the entire manuscript but also continued to encourage me to get this work published by his unwavering support.

I began writing this book in Nairobi, Kenya at the Jesuit Loyola House. I finished this work at the Jesuit School of Theology in Berkeley, CA, Chardin House. I would like to thank the residents of these two houses who provided a conducive atmosphere for me to write. A special thank you goes to two residents of Chardin House: Randy Gibbens, SJ and Luke Hansen, SJ for their interest in this story.

Finally, I would like to thank my mum Francesca and my dad Richard for their love and support.

Oscar Momanyi
Berkeley, California
November 6, 2017

Map of South Sudan

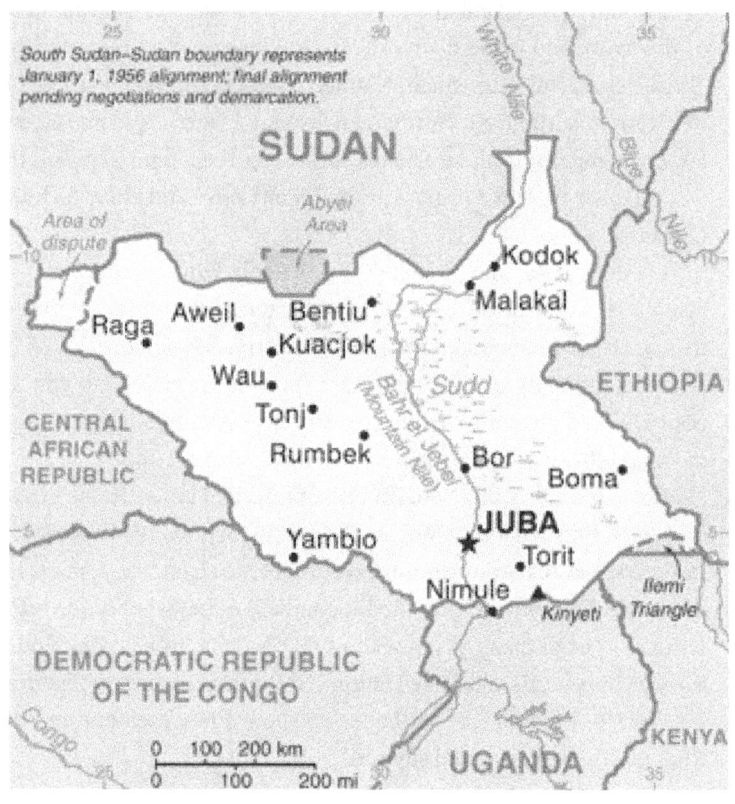

Map courtesy of
https://www.cia.gov/library/publications/the-world-factbook/geos/od.html.

National Anthem of South Sudan

Oh God
We praise and glorify You
For Your grace on South Sudan,
The land of great abundance
Uphold us united in peace and harmony.
Oh motherland
We rise raising flag with the guiding star
And sing songs of freedom with joy;
For justice, liberty and prosperity
Shall forever more reign.
Oh great patriots
Let us stand up in silence and respect,
Saluting our martyrs whose blood
Cemented our national foundation,
We vow to protect our nation.
Oh God, bless South Sudan.

Chapter One

On the Threshold of Hope

"Yahweh said to Abram, 'Leave your country, your family and your father's house, for the land I will show you."

Genesis 12:1

One theme that captivates Pope Francis is solidarity with the people in the margins of society. In *Evangelii Gaudium* (EG) or *The Joy of the Gospel*, Pope Francis succinctly asks that, "Each Christian and every community must discern the path that the Lord points out, but all of us are asked to obey His call to go forth from our own comfort zone in order to reach all the "peripheries" in need of the light of the Gospel" (EG 20). The companions of Jesus, also known as the Jesuits, have always been in the frontiers which Pope Francis speaks about in EG. I was privileged to work, as part of my Jesuit training, in such a frontier in the war-torn South Sudan for two years (2012-2014). The following is a story of witness to the message of Christ in Matthew 28:19, "Go therefore and make disciples of all nations, baptizing them in the name of the Father and of the

Son and of the Holy Spirit."

One evening in Wau, South Sudan, after hard labor at Loyola Secondary School in the often unforgiving heat, four Jesuits gathered for a Eucharistic celebration in their little chapel. They were celebrating the memorial of Saint Peter Canisius that great Jesuit apostle of Germany in the sixteenth century. After the readings from the scriptures were done, one of the Jesuits present recounted the life of that indefatigable apostle of Germany. Peter Canisius is among the great forefathers of the Society of Jesus. The life of the Saint evoked a lot of emotions in the Jesuits present at that Mass and there followed a chain of testimonies about the heroic work the Jesuits had done in the Sudan and the new nation South Sudan. They were truly following in the footsteps of that iconic Jesuit Saint, albeit in a different time and context. That Eucharistic sacrifice serves as the basis of the adventures that will unfold in the following pages.

* * *

The Baganda people of Uganda have a proverb that says, "if you want to know the gender of a tortoise, put it in the fire!" When I got news about my assignment to South Sudan, I felt I was about to be placed in the fire! South Sudan was going to be a difficult one. Jesuits are usually assigned to specific ministries after a long period of discernment and prayer. Although I had done my discernment for several months, by accepting my mission to South Sudan, I still felt unsure of what to expect. I felt that I was being put to the test, like a Baganda tortoise, and I had to seek God's help to withstand the challenges that were ahead of me. I knew that I was going into another world altogether than the one I was used to. South Sudan is a country with a traumatized past, a trauma which continues to bedevil it. I accepted the mission with fear and trembling, yet I trusted that God would lead me every step of the way.

A beautiful incident happened before my departure to the frontier of South Sudan which gave me a lot of hope and inspiration. On Tuesday, July 17, 2012, the 70th Congregation of Procurators (CP 70) ended with a Mass at the chapel of *Mwangaza* (Shining Light) Retreat Center in the Karen area of Nairobi, Kenya. CP 70 was a meeting of Jesuits from all over the world that takes place every four years. That was the first time that the meeting took place in Africa and, thus, it was a special occasion for all the Jesuits who took part in it.

During the CP 70, Fr. Adolfo Nicolas, SJ the former Superior General of the Society of Jesus, gave a speech on the state of the global Society of Jesus (*De Statu Societis Iesu*). In that speech, he emphasized the need for Jesuits to go to the "frontiers" where other people do not want to go. This was an iteration of General Congregation (GC) 35 of the Society of Jesus which took place in 2008. GC 35 brought the idea of going to the frontiers in a more forceful way to the consciousness of the Jesuits all over the world. South Sudan constituted a frontier for the Jesuits of Eastern Africa, and I was happy to be among the people going to that peripheral region. I felt that the words of Fr. Nicolas were directly addressed to me. I felt that I was on the brink of responding to the "preferential option for the poor" in a radical way. That thought gave me a lot of joy and hope.

* * *

Before embarking on my new mission in South Sudan, I got a lot of encouragement from many friends who understood the difficulty of the task ahead of me. Others simply sympathized with me; they saw what lay ahead of me as a tragedy. I had to focus on the positive side of the mission: even if it is a difficult mission, I was going to make a difference in the lives of people whose needs were greatest. This idea gave me hope and strength of mind.

Travelling to South Sudan was the first worry that was in my mind for several weeks before my departure. On the eve of my departure from Nairobi, Kenya to Rumbek, South Sudan, I was informed that I was not able to get a seat in the United Nations Humanitarian Air Service (UNHAS) chartered flight. This flight was the most reliable one going to South Sudan at that time. For this reason, I was ready to stay two more days in Nairobi so that I could arrange again for another UNHAS flight. However, the Jesuit who was organizing my travels told me that we could somehow find a flight for the following day.

After supper that evening, the Jesuit told me to get ready to go to Wilson Airport, a small ramshackle airport on the fringes of Nairobi, to check with some pilots there if there were chartered planes that were going to Rumbek the following day. When we arrived at the office of a flight company simply known as ALS Limited, we found out that it was closed. ALS was the most reliable way of getting into South Sudan after the UNHAS flights.

We were so disillusioned, but we decided to check out a restaurant, which was inside the airport compound. My Jesuit companion knew that some pilots who flew small chartered planes spent their evenings at that restaurant, and one could speak to them and inquire if there were free seats in their planes going to South Sudan the following day. These pilots wielded a lot of power over who could get into their planes or not. Unfortunately, we were not able to see any pilot around there. We ended up inquiring from a security guard who was there. He advised us to come back to the airport the following morning with my bags. If we got a seat, then I would go to Rumbek; if not I would stay for a few more days in Nairobi. That is how my journey of trusting that all was in God's hands began. My friend told me to pack my bags that night, but I was not to be too sure that I would depart the next day. I was embarking on a journey whose future urged me to hope against hope.

Early next morning, we went again to Wilson Airport. There were many aid workers at the airport. Most of them knew each other, and they were having animated conversations. They were mostly Africans with a few Europeans and Americans. They seemed to have had a feeling of camaraderie amongst themselves; they were happy. Most of them had badges for identifying them. A good number of them were going to northern Kenya, which is an impoverished area while a few were on their way to South Sudan and Somalia. As I sat there, I had a feeling that I was about to enter a totally different world.

When the ALS desk was opened the Jesuit accompanying me went to inquire if I could get a seat on their morning flight. After a short while, the Jesuit came back and told me that there was a seat for me, but we had to wait. I was exhilarated; I did not want to wait anymore. I wanted to be in South Sudan as soon as I could.

A few minutes later a man came to where we sat and asked

us to go to the counter. They weighed my luggage and found it to be thirty-five kilograms. They only accepted twenty kilograms for both carry on and checked in luggage. Hence, we had to pay five US dollars for each extra kilogram. I had already reduced my luggage in an ingenious and shocking way: I wore three trousers, three t-shirts, two shirts, a jacket, and a coat; yet I still had extra luggage. One of the trousers had side pockets in which I had stashed some small books and other things.

After waiting for about an hour, a man of Asian origin quickly came in and called us to board the plane. The plane was very small, and we had to bend over in order to enter through a small door. The plane had a capacity of about 20 passengers. We were 12 passengers and some other seats had small cargo on them. The flight deck was open, and I could see how the pilots maneuvered the plane.

We were airborne after about ten minutes of boarding. The plane was very unstable in the air. It swerved up and down, and at one point I felt that we were going to crash only to see the plane rise a few seconds later, and it continued cruising. About half way through the flight there was heavy rainfall which made visibility difficult, but we just continued the course. The pilots were in total control of the plane, and that assured us that we were safe. As we approached the northern Kenya town of Lokichoggio, popularly known as Loki, I saw many mountain ranges with very sharp rock formations. The pilots negotiated the plane through these with a lot of precision before landing at Loki. We were lucky that the rain had reduced, and the visibility had improved. With the heavy rain, I thought that we were going to hit a mountain range, I was scared to the bones, but still, I felt God's abiding presence with me.

Loki is found in Turkanaland, an impoverished part of northern Kenya. The poverty there is similar to that of South Sudan. It is home to the Turkana people, who are nomadic pastoralists. Loki is a transit point for many chartered planes going into South Sudan and Turkanaland. Many NGOs working in these areas prefer to fly to Loki because most roads that come up to Lodwar town, which is the hub of the northern part of Kenya, are in a very bad condition. From Loki, it is easy to travel by road within northern Kenya by use of Land Rovers and Land Cruisers.

The flight from Nairobi to Loki was about fifty minutes. After landing, we were asked to get out so that the plane could be refueled. I walked to a little house about two hundred meters from the plane to take shelter because it was still raining. The area around the airport had tall grass, but the little airport was nice and with a smooth run way. I sat there on a bench under a small shed on the periphery of the runway watching a good omen. There was rain in the desert of Turkana country. This was a sign that my life in South Sudan would be grace filled. I did not go to the immigration at Loki because I had finished all my immigration issues at Wilson Airport in Nairobi. There was a restaurant and a duty-free shop near the immigration at Loki. Both were quite expensive, and so I did not buy anything there at that time.

Lokichoggio Airport is a civilian airport that serves the town of Loki and surrounding communities. The airport is home to one of the largest and longest running humanitarian aid projects. Global aid projects are run by aid groups such as the UNICEF, and The World Food Program (WFP) to South Sudan and to neighboring areas within Kenya. The South Sudanese Catholic Diocese of Torit (DOT) has an operation center at

Loki, which helps coordinate the flow of goods and personnel into the inaccessible parts of DOT.

I was happy to be there in Loki at that time. I felt a sense of exhilaration and that God was confirming me in the mission that I was about to undertake. I gave thanks to God and felt God's presence reassuring me that all will be well. I had a feeling of total abandonment to God's will. We spent about thirty minutes at Loki with rain and cold breezes. Then we were told to prepare for boarding. I went to be parted down by a young man who was shocked by the amount of clothing that was on my body. He asked me if I did not feel hot inside the plane. I ignored his question, I went straight back into the plane, and I took off my jacket and coat.

Chapter Two

Entering Canaan

"Then Yahweh said to Moses, 'Now I will rain down bread for you from the heavens. Each day the people are to go out and gather the day's portion."

Exodus 16:4

I was exhilarated when I first entered South Sudan. I was in so much fear but at the same time with so much hope that God was going to be present in all that I was going to do. I had mixed feelings, something similar to that of the Israelites in the wilderness on their way to Canaan narrated in the book of Exodus. I knew that I was in God's hands and that I would always rely in God's providence in the challenges that were ahead.

After the stop at Loki, we embarked on the last leg of our journey. It was a smoother ride than the first leg from Nairobi to Loki. Within an hour, we were at Rumbek Airport. When we approached Rumbek, I could see from the air as the plane was descending, some little lakes scattered all over the terrain. I later learned that Rumbek was found in the Lakes Region, which is translated as *Al-Buhayrat* in Arabic, and the region is perhaps named after those little lakes.

The runway at Rumbek Airport was made of dirt, and yet it was level, and without potholes, the landing was very smooth. If Wilson Airport was ramshackle, Rumbek Airport was even more rundown. There was a small two-roomed house that served as immigration offices. There were many UN helicopters at the airport. My first impression was that there was a huge UN presence in South Sudan. I later learned that that was a UN airport used solely for humanitarian purposes, but it was gradually handed over to the government. The commercial planes landing there were required to pay a fee. A year after my arrival, an ALS plane was held at that airport for hours because the owners had defaulted in paying the required airport fees which amounted to thousands of South Sudanese Pounds (SSP).

As we got out of the plane at Rumbek Airport, I experienced a sudden rush of hot air, a heat wave on my face. It was extremely hot; about 105 degrees farenheight! I had never experienced such heat in my life. The clothes I was putting on made things even worse. I longed to get home so that I could get off all the clothes.

All the passengers walked across the dirt runway to the tiny immigration office at one end of the airport. Some people were waiting to receive the newly arrived. Some aid workers were quickly picked up by their friends, and they left the airport immediately. There were some South Sudanese soldiers and police there who looked at the newly arrived with inquisitive eyes. I looked around for a young Jesuit who was supposed to pick me up from the airport, but I did not see him. All the faces there were unfamiliar to me; I felt scared for a moment. I went and sat on a bench near the immigration office and waited for my luggage to be hauled out of the plane.

After about ten minutes; an elderly white man, in his mid-seventies, came towards me. I thought the man just wanted to chat with me because I looked different from the other Dinka people who were standing there. He asked me, "Are you from Loyola House, Nairobi?" I quickly answered, "Yes." He introduced himself as Br. Herbert Liebl, SJ one of the Jesuits working in Rumbek. He is an Austrian national and had worked in Rumbek since the early 2000s. He had come to receive me at the airport. He immediately welcomed me and said, "I know you are going to the school in Wau, but don't get stuck in teaching." He went on to say that there were more important ministries than teaching. He emphasized that being with the people and helping them to grow spiritually in a parish setting is better than teaching high school. We had a short spiritual conversation, which he initiated, and I could immediately sense that he was a man of spiritual depth. I immediately felt God amazing embrace of me through that humble and spiritual man who stood in front of me.

Br. Liebl had worked elsewhere in Africa (Angola and Liberia) with the Jesuit Refuge Service (JRS). He found his work with JRS satisfying. He had particularly fond memories of his work among the Vietnamese refugees in Palou Bidong Island where he worked before he came to Africa.

Palou Bidong is a one square kilometer island which is situated off the coast of Terengganu, Malaysia in the South China Sea. In 1975, the Vietnam War ended with the fall of Saigon to the North Vietnamese army. Millions of people tried to flee the new communist rule in Vietnam. In May 1975, the first boat with 47 Vietnamese "boat people" arrived in Malaysia. Palou Bidong was officially opened as a refugee camp on August 8, 1978, with 121 Vietnamese refugees. Br. Liebl arrived there to work with JRS in 1989. JRS was founded in 1980 by Fr. Pedro Arrupe, SJ partly because the plight of the Vietnamese "boat people" highlighted a great need for accompanying the refugees. The way Br. Liebl described his arrival in Palou Bidong in 1989 was very moving:

> "I arrived in boat number MC139. As I found out later, I took the same boat to Palou Bidong together with my first interpreter, Ms. Phuong Le Quynh. In her, I found not only a wonderful interpreter but a friend. I arrived as an outsider but was welcomed by the whole Vietnamese refugee community. I experienced the most fascinating work I ever had in my life. I worked for the unaccompanied minors from Vietnam, children between 3 to 14 years. I shared the assignment with Sr. Nancy from the USA. Sr. Nancy took care of the minors in the open camp, and I was in charge of small families and took care of the kids. From the community, we got foster parents who took care the kids. Most of them had a Buddhist background. I was fascinated by the way these Vietnamese people took care of their children. We organized music lessons, played games and we made a schedule for cooking, cleaning and other activities. We wanted to create a space for these youngsters so that they could feel safe, and in a way, feel at home. Those kids missed their parents and thus many tears and pain were daily companions to

these little ones. I loved them and still love them more than my life."[1]

Br. Liebl's witness among the "boat people" inspired me to be a witness to the South Sudanese people. He was a man for others, totally dedicated to the service of God's people. I felt so welcomed by God through the generous life of Br. Liebl. At the time, I met him in July 2012, Br. Liebl served in various capacities at the Jesuit mission in Rumbek: he was the administrator of the Jesuit house, and was renovating the house and the Jesuit church. He also did spiritual ministries around Rumbek. He had started a series of Small Christian Communities (SCCs) in the villages around Rumbek town, which he followed up closely. SCCs were common in other places of East Africa but not in South Sudan and therefore Br. Liebl was addressing an area of great need. He would walk for long distances every afternoon in order to go to the meetings of these communities that happened in the Dinka households.

He built the Jesuit house in Rumbek in 2002. It was a difficult job to get the building materials from Kenya and Uganda because they were not available in Rumbek. Several times the lorries carrying the building materials disappeared for months. He had to travel many kilometers in the rough terrain to retrieve the materials in the forests of South Sudan's Equatoria region.

* * *

After finishing with the immigration, at Rumbek Airport, Br. Liebl drove us in a little Land Cruiser to St. Teresa Mission of

---

[1] Reflection by Br. Herbert Liebl on his experience in Palou Bidong.

Reconciliation Church. This church is in the same compound with the St. Peter Claver Jesuit Community. It was a ten minutes' drive from Rumbek Airport. We passed through some grass thatched Dinka houses, and I saw, for the first time, the long-horned Dinka cows. It was a fascinating scene. I had never seen such cows. The cows were mostly brown. There were a few white and black ones. I learned later that those white and black cows were very precious to the Dinka people. Anyone who had one of these was respected. Additionally, a cow with twisted horns was also held in high esteem.

The grass thatched houses, with walls made of mud, were peculiarly well done. These houses were locally known as *tukuls*. They were built better that the ones I had seen in Kenya and Zimbabwe. They were a work of art done with precision and care and had beautiful patterns engraved on them. These *tukuls* were different from *raqubas*, which were entirely made of grass reeds and bamboo sticks.

"Come follow me" (Matthew 4:9) kept reverberating in my mind as I began to get into the "real life" of the South Sudanese people. These words of Jesus reminded me of my original desire to be a follower of Jesus in whatever circumstance I find myself. I was encountering a new culture, and I was feeling overwhelmed, but the idea that I was following in the footsteps of Jesus was consoling.

* * *

A word about the Dinka found in Rumbek: they are a special clan of the Dinka people known as the Agaar. The Agaar are said to be the fiercest among the twenty-two Dinka clans. The clans usually engage in cattle raiding escapades. Notable Dinka people include the late Dr. John Garang de Mabior, who was the leader of the Sudan People's Liberation Movement/Army (SPLM/A) and Vice President of the Sudan, Salva Kiir Mayardit the first President of South Sudan, Loul Deng and the late Manute Bol both of the National Basketball Association (NBA). Abel Alier, who was once the Vice President of Sudan between 1971 to 1982 and is an astute lawyer. Others include super models Awek Lek and Mari Malek in New York, Francis Mading Deng, who is a writer, diplomat at the UN in New York and a distinguished scholar.

The Nuer, Shilluk, Azande, Lotuko, Bari and the Anuak are the other significant ethnic groups found in South Sudan. In general, the Dinka found in South Sudan refer to themselves as *Jieng* or *Muonyjang*. Legend has it that the name Dinka came up in the following way: the eauropean explorers who first met the Jieng in the 18th century could not pronounce the name, and so they corrupted the name of a Jieng chief, Deng Kak, into Dinka. The Dinka occupy an area covering central Jonglei region on the eastern bank of Nile River stretching northwest of northern Bahr el Ghazal to the western Bahr el Ghazal. They are found mostly in the midst of many small streams and rivers that feed into the main River Nile.

The total population of the Dinka was estimated to be in the range of 2.5 to 3 million according to a 2008 census. This figure makes the Dinka be the largest ethnic group in South Sudan whose total population is estimated to be 12 million according to the census mentioned above. During my stay in South Sudan, it seemed to me that the Dinka dominated all walks of life, and this made the other ethnic communities loath them.

* * *

My impression of Rumbek at that time: most of the buildings were semi-permanent (made of mud), but they were arranged in an orderly manner. It appeared to me like a village market rather than a town, although there were signs that it was being modernized. It seemed to me that the central market was the main business area in the whole of the town. Most of the traders in that market were Ugandans; I could tell that from their accents. There were also a few Kenyans. I learned that very often these traders were harassed by some police officers. It was said that even Dinka civilians sometimes threated the Ugandan traders. The locals had a feeling that the foreigners from Kenya and Uganda were taking up their valuable jobs. At that time in Rumbek, I was told that one Ugandan trader had his shop forcibly closed and it was later taken up by a Dinka.

After the signing of the Comprehensive Peace Agreement (CPA) in 2005, the SPLM chose Rumbek to serve as a temporary administrative headquarters for the government of Southern Sudan. Reporting for the BBC in January 2005 Jonah Fisher filed the following report from Rumbek:

> "With no multistory buildings or paved roads and a population of under 100,000, the ramshackle town of Rumbek has been chosen by Sudan's former southern rebels as the unlikely administrative capital of the south. But there is plenty of optimism around the town, with the peace deal, which gives the south a greater say in running its affairs, still fresh in the memory. "Rumbek will be like a small London," Makok, a smiling legal officer, told me as he gave us a lift on the back of his motorbike - one of the few in

town. [...] But the reality for the town is that although peace has finally come after 21 years of civil war, almost everything will have to be built from scratch. The airstrip is a dirt track where goats graze alongside the rusting remains of an aircraft which once crash-landed. The brick buildings along the untarred roads are now empty shells - testament to the intense fighting the area saw during the war, which left an estimated 1.5 million dead. People live in traditional thatched huts and hardly anyone has electricity or running water. "There has been no rebuilding because we only reached a [peace] settlement the other day," said Gordon Mapel, an administrator from the Sudanese People's Liberation Movement (SPLM). "We are going to have roads; we are going to have roofs; we are going to have nice buildings."" [2]

Rumbek served as the administrative capital for a while before the government headquarters were moved to Juba. Juba was more developed and accessible by road from the other East African countries. It also had a good airport. Rumbek served as a temporary capital because, after the CPA, the soldiers for the government in Khartoum, Sudan continued to occupy Juba for a few months.

The vice of prostitution had begun to raise its ugly head in the town of Rumbek at the time of my arrival there. This was a new phenomenon in a society which had strict sexual norms and traditions. In the news around Rumbek at that time was that the Governor of the area was complaining that the

---

[2] Jonah Fisher, "South Sudan's unlikely capital" BBC NEWS Friday, 21 January 2005, 12:09 GMT http://news.bbc.co.uk/2/hi/africa/4192133.stm.

foreigners, mainly Ugandans and Kenyans, had brought HIV/AIDS to Rumbek, and there was a crackdown that was ongoing on these prostitutes.

* * *

In my first tour of Rumbek town, as we drove from the Jesuit community to the main market, we passed the Independence or Freedom Square. This is where, one year earlier on July 9, 2011, the independence or the birth of the new nation South Sudan was celebrated. The illustrious Bishop Caesar Mazzolari, MCCJ of the Catholic Diocese of Rumbek took part in the celebrations. He gave a moving speech and officiated the prayers on that day. This was a few days before he suffered a heart attack and died while attending Mass at Rumbek Cathedral on July 16, 2011 (more about him below).

The Independence Square had some facilities such as a basketball court, a netball court, etc., where young people would meet in the evenings to engage sporting activities. Other young people would just congregate there to socialize on Sundays and during public holidays. Some others engaged in informal fashion shows where they would wear Western clothes, and they would move around showing off. This was a new phenomenon in Rumbek. Westernization was first invading that rather traditional and somewhat closed society. The Independence Square played the function of bringing people together which was very important for the young nation.

In the environs of Rumbek, there were camps for the returnees who had come back to the south after the separation of the country from Sudan in 2011. Most of the people in these camps had lost their belongings during their transfer from the north. The government was trying to provide for their necessities, but the conditions in the camps remained dire. Fr. Francis Njuguna, SJ, a Jesuit who was working in Rumbek at that time had visited these camps a couple of times to be with the people. Several NGOs were working there at that time.

There were also cattle camps, on the outskirts of Rumbek town, in which thousands upon thousands of cattle belonging to particular Dinka clans were found. The Dinka people are a cattle-keeping folk. Dinka life revolves around cows. Cattle keeping is a way of life for them. The life in the cattle camps was hard. Young boys of about 7 to 12 years old were the ones in charge of taking care of the cows. They usually had guns which they used for protecting the cows from invaders. They slept among the cows. At night, they smeared themselves with cow dung to prevent them from being bitten by mosquitoes. In the mornings, they would use cattle urine to clean their faces because of the scarcity of water.

These boys were hardened by this tough life until they graduated into adulthood when they were about twelve years old. After passing through the cattle camp experience, they underwent scarification in which some peculiar marks were inscribed on their faces. These marks would distinguish members of one clan or ethnic group from another. The marks were also a sign that a person had successfully completed the rites of passage and had become a man. The rites of passage included the cattle camp experience which was a crucial moment.

Men of other ethnic groups in South Sudan such as Nuer and the Jur (Luo) also had scars on their faces, but these scars differed according to ethnic groups. The culture of scarification was slowly dying out during my stay in South Sudan. Some

Dinka students at Loyola Secondary School had these scars on their faces while some did not. I asked some who did not have why that was the case, and they told me that "those things are now outdated!"

Even amidst such poverty and challenges that Rumbek posed, I could see that the people there were happy, and they went on with their lives normally. I had made a vow of poverty when I finished my first two years of Jesuit training. However, standing in Rumbek that day, poverty took a whole different dimension. I kept asking myself: How can I live my vow of poverty in a more radical way, in a way that can be more freeing that can lead to a happiness that abundance cannot provide? The people of Rumbek were teaching me the true meaning of the beatitude "Blessed are the poor in spirit: for theirs is the kingdom of Heaven" (Matthew 5:3).

* * *

In the morning of the day after my arrival in Rumbek, we celebrated the holy Eucharist at the community chapel with Fr. Njuguna presiding. The chapel was small but very nice. It was painted white on the inside, and some flowers were nicely around the sacred altar, a sign of hope for the new country. Br. Liebl served as the sacristan, and he was there doing his prayers before the Mass. He was a model of "man for others" trusting and serving with all his heart.

The Eucharist was going to the center of my life since the situation I had entered called for absolute fidelity to the tender care and love of God that I could only get at the Eucharist and through my prayers. I could tell that the other Jesuits there were totally dedicated to their prayers and to the Eucharist. I felt close to God at that my first eucharistic celebration in South Sudan: I felt called to be an instrument of peace, joy, and love to the people there who have endured decades of suffering.

Br. Liebl also baked some tasty bread that was popular in the Jesuit community in Rumbek. To get fresh bread in Rumbek town was pretty difficult. Thus, it was a relief to have the bread that Br. Liebl baked. I spent that morning resting and doing some reading. Br. Liebl told me to take it easy, and enter into the new situation slowly. "South Sudan is not a place to rush into, take your time," he said. I found him to be very encouraging.

* * *

At that time, I was eager to visit the Catholic cathedral of Rumbek. It was a small old church which was built in the 1950s. There were ongoing plans for building a new cathedral. I was shown a small wooden house, in the compound where the diocesan offices were found, in which the Jesuits lived when they came to Rumbek in early 2000. Fr. Salvador Ferrão, SJ, a Goan Jesuit was the first Jesuit to arrive in Rumbek (more about him later).

During that tour of the cathedral compound, I also saw the small one roomed house in which the late Bishop Caesar Mazzolari, MCCJ lived. It had only a bed and a working table. He used it as his bedroom and office. The Bishop was earlier living in a thatched house, a *tukul*. After his death in 2011, Bishop Mazzolari was buried in the cathedral church in Rumbek.

The *Catholic News Service* reported on his death on July 18, 2011, in the following way:

"The bishop fell backward, clutching his chest and gasping for air, at the beginning of the consecration. He was pronounced dead at a local hospital. Catholics from the diocese recalled Bishop Mazzolari as a zealous worker who reopened missions and negotiated humanitarian assistance for the diocese. He also promoted education and health care and "passionately responded to human need at every level," they said. "Like St. Paul, Bishop Mazzolari spent his life at the service of the Gospel, always assuring us that God was journeying with the people of South Sudan," said a statement released by diocesan Catholics. "His fatherly care and compassion, generosity and selflessness were sources of hope and comfort to all those he encountered." They recalled how the bishop presided over the opening prayer of the Independence Day Celebration in Rumbek July 9, 2011. He was "moved with tears of joy to see the jubilation of the people of Southern Sudan at the referendum.""[3]

Bishop Mazzolari was a Comboni Missionary. The Comboni Missionaries are considered to be the pioneers of evangelization in the Sudan. The congregation was founded by Saint Daniele Comboni in Italy. Bishop Mazzolari was born in Brescia, Italy in 1937. He was ordained a Comboni priest in San Diego, California on March 17, 1962. He spent 19 years working among African-American and Mexican mine workers in Cincinnati, Ohio. In 1981, he moved to the Sudanese

---

[3] See "Bishop Mazzolari of Rumbek, South Sudan, dies during Mass" *Catholic News Service*, July 18, 2011.
http://www.catholicnews.com/data/stories/cns/1102843.htm.

Diocese of Tombura-Yambio at the invitation of Bishop Joseph Abangite Gasi. In 1990, he was appointed Apostolic Administrator of the Diocese of Rumbek. He was consecrated Bishop of Rumbek in 1999.

* * *

In Genesis chapter twelve, Abram left his country with fear and trembling on the way to the unknown. I had a similar feeling as a fellow Jesuit drove me to the Rumbek bus station to get transportation to Wau, my final destination. At the bus station I was to get a Land Cruiser that would take me to the unknown. I hoped for the best. There were many people at the bus station. It was an utterly chaotic place full of all kinds of riffraff. Beggars were moving around with their haggard faces asking for money. They would stick their hands through the windows of cars asking for help from the passengers. There were gangs of glue-sniffing boys who just hanged around there doing nothing. They seemed to be very hostile. There were soldiers and police there too. Many people were wearing army and police uniforms and were carrying guns; I was surprised. Were all those people police officers or army men?

The journey to Wau was rough. I was lucky I got a comfortable seat just behind the driver. Sitting at the back of the Land Cruiser could have been very uncomfortable. I was to experience that later on. We saw many checkpoints on the way, but I was lucky that I was not checked as I had expected. Most of the checkpoints were manned by the SPLA soldiers. The checkpoints were mainly small semi-permanent houses (*raqubas*) constructed by the use of grass reeds and bamboo trees found on the roadside, sometimes as close as twenty kilometers from each other.

The only people who were checked, on that journey, were a couple of police officers who travelled with us. They were in full police attire, and some of them travelled with their guns. It seemed to me that there was a suspicion that some people were impersonating police officers, and that was why the police officers travelling in our car had to produce documents to authenticate their identity in order to be allowed to pass through the checkpoints. I wondered why they wore their uniforms, yet they were not on duty. I learned later that in South Sudan, rank was very important. To wear a uniform, especially police or army uniforms, gave someone his or her credentials and status in the society. I remember some of the parents at Loyola Secondary School who would come in full military or police attire to the school in order to intimidate the teachers.

The countryside was mainly made up of forested areas with sparse population. Wreckage of broken cars could be seen all through the journey. I prayed that our car would not break down because we could be stuck in that jungle for several days. I had heard stories of some passengers who had spent up to three days on that road because their car broke down.

There were also many soldiers scattered across the countryside as we drove through. It looked like we were driving through a war zone. I always felt scared when we approached a group of military men; they looked terrifying.

The people in the car spoke in Arabic and, thus, I could not follow their conversations since I did not know Arabic. They kept repeating the word *arabia,* and I thought that they were saying that I did not know Arabic. I later learned that the word means a car in Arabic; then I concluded they were generally speaking about cars. At some checkpoints, the driver was required to pay a fee.

We stopped, after about five hours of travelling, for lunch in the timeworn town of Tonj. It looked like an old colonial town, part of it was built by the use of bricks. Another part had dilapidated semi-permanent houses. Tonj is located on the edge of a small river. It is the largest town in the Warap region of South Sudan. It is home to the Dinka Rek people, a clan of the Dinka. The Luo (Jur) and the Bongo ethnic groups also reside in Tonj. The people of Tonj grow crops and raise livestock. In the town's central market, foodstuffs such as vegetables and other basic goods were sold daily. Tonj is a key town along the main trade route from Uganda heading north of South Sudan.

I had not seen such depravity in my life as the one I saw in Tonj at that time. Life seemed to be reduced to bear minimum. A lot of dust floated in the air. The poverty there seemed dire. The driver stopped the car near a line of shops along the main road where everyone got out. I felt dizzy as I got out because of being thrown left, right and center in the car on that rough road. I went to a nearby shop, which had a Ugandan shopkeeper, I could judge that from his accent. When I arrived at that shop, the shopkeeper quickly got out a mat and went on his knees to say his midday prayers; he was a Muslim. I was surprised to witness this, I had never seen such a spectacle in my life and I said a little prayer although I felt very tired. He spent about five minutes in prayer. I then bought some snacks, and I sat down and began to eat.

We finally arrived in Wau town after passing across a large old bridge over the Jur River. There was a sentry post that manned the bridge, we stopped there for another check. The bridge had light posts on both sides and was paved, a sign of a more developed area. I was later told a story of how the people on the eastern bank of the Jur River were captivated by those lights during the long gone glorious days of Wau when the town had electricity. These people would stand there at night marveling at the impressive lights over the bridge!

During that journey through that unknown land, I did feel scared, but I did not feel abandoned by God. God continued to show me God's love and kindness through the smiles of the people I saw and just by the fact that I was with other people in the journey. I was not travelling in that pilgrimage alone, but with God and others even though I was clearly in a difficult journey. The poverty was extreme, yet the people were not brought down by that fact. The people were full of hope, and that gave me a lot of inspiration. I asked God to help me do some good for the people there and also to learn from them too.

Chapter Three

Trusting in the Slow Work of God

"Above all, trust in the slow work of God. We are quite naturally impatient in everything to reach the end without delay. Give our Lord the benefit of believing that His hand is leading you."

Teilhard de Chardin, SJ

"Where in South Sudan are you going to live?" inquired a friend. "I am going to stay Wau," I answered. She immediately exclaimed, "wow you are going to Wau!" I felt relieved as I stood in Wau for the first time. The difficult travel was over, and at last, I had arrived at my destiny for the next few years. The journey to Wau had been long and torturous, but I was happy. Driving or travelling in public Land Cruisers through South Sudan was a horrendous experience during the dry season because of the dust. After travelling on those roads for about two hours, the amount of dust one inhaled was incredible! It was common to see people covered with dust as they arrived after a day's journey. It was a very interesting scene! As I stood in Wau for the first time covered in dust, I was filled with an ironic cheerfulness. To travel during the rainy season was equally bad. There was a high chance a car could get stuck on the muddy roads for days.

There were many permanent houses in the town of Wau, they all looked so dusty. Our car went straight into Wau market popularly known as Souk Wau. A souk is a bazaar or a market in the Arabic language. All passengers got out of the car, and I followed suit. A little boy, who was perhaps 12 or 13 years old, approached me, looked at me curiously, and told me; *mzee habari* by which he meant: how are you, old man? He was trying to speak to me in broken Swahili because he realized that I was not a South Sudanese from my complexion. Most South Sudanese are of dark complexion while I have lighter skin. The boy guessed that I may be a Kenyan or Ugandan. He asked me politely if he could get my luggage from the top of the car. His kindness moved me, and I accepted the offer. Afterwards, I gave him 5 South Sudanese Pounds. He was overjoyed and thanked me with all his heart.

The boy's behavior was very surprising considering the hostile treatment I had received from some rowdy boys I met at Rumbek bus station. That boy's conduct made me feel welcomed. He was Godsent, through his gracious welcome I felt that God was going to be favorable to me in Wau! I immediately had a feeling that Wau people were hospitable. The bus stop in Wau had some order compared to the one in Rumbek.

I carried my bags to a secluded place to get away from drivers of Indian style motorbikes which had been converted into small passenger taxis. These drivers came in flooding towards me asking if I wanted their services. I told them I was waiting for someone to pick me up, but they did not understand what I said because they did not know English and they continued pestering me in Arabic. I also did not understand what they said. The Indian style converted motorcycles are known as *rakshas* in that part of the world. These converted motorbikes were the major means of transport in the town of Wau. I think that the name *raksha* is borrowed from the Indian rickshaw.

I took a quick *raksha* ride to Jebel Kheir, a suburb in the western part of Wau, where the Jesuit community and school were located. I was surprised to see how modest Loyola Secondary School was. It was not like other Jesuit schools that I had seen elsewhere. I was equally shocked to see the tall grass that was in the surroundings. I arrived in the middle of the rainy season a time when to control the growth of grass in that tropical climate was very difficult. The grass kept growing all the time.

* * *

The first impression I had of Wau town was that it was more developed than Rumbek. It had a semblance of an urban area. There was a tarmac road on one side of town although it was not in good condition. Electric poles were coming from a little diesel engine power station which was on one part of the town. That station had stopped its operations many years before my arrival. The people of Wau were comely and hospitable. Arabic was widely spoken, and it was the medium of instruction in most of the schools. The temperature was almost the same as the one I had experienced in Rumbek. It was very hot; the maximum temperature was around forty degrees Celsius during the day and twenty-seven degrees Celsius during the night.

Wau was initially established as a fortified base (a *zariba* in

Arabic) by slave traders in the early 19th century. It was part of a vast network of the trans-Saharan slaving activities. Comboni Missionary Fr. Stefano Santandrea, MCCJ, who lived in Wau during the Anglo-Egyptian Condominium Rule (1898-1956), observed in his *A Popular History of Wau: From Its Foundations to About 1940* that the origin of the name Wau is contested. However, Fr. Santandrea opines that Wau was likely named by the Dinka, who migrated into the area from the eastern bank of the Jur River. These Dinkas settled north of Wau and were famous for naming the places where they passed through unlike other ethnic groups found in the area.[4]

Wau was taken over from the slave traders by the French during the latter's brief occupation of Bahr el-Ghazal in the 1890s. During the French occupation, the town was known as *Fort Desaix*. The French left Wau in 1900. At that time, the town resembled a settlement rather than a town. The Anglo-Egyptian authorities annexed Wau in 1901. During the Anglo-Egyptian rule, Wau became an administrative center of the Bahr el Ghazal region.

In *Requiem for the Sudan: War and Disaster Relief in the Nile*, J. Millard Burr, and Robert O. Collins described Wau in the following way:

> "No one has ever been "at home" in Wau. Situated on the fringe of the Dinka country, it is surrounded by a host of disorganized and diverse peoples. The British occupied Wau on 17 January 1901 but never knew whether it was a Dinka town, an Azande village, or the abode of the Sudanic cultivators crushed between these two dynamic African peoples.

---

[4] Stefano Santandrea. *A Popular History of Wau: From Its Foundations to About 1940*. Unpublished Manuscript, Rome: 1977, 2.

Malakal and Juba, situated on the right and left banks of the Nile, respectively, were explicable polities, Wau was an aberration. It was and remains a town belonging to no single ethnic group, deriving its importance only from its position as a commercial and administrative center at the confluence of the Bussere and Sue Rivers. Located in the midst of the vast Nilotic plain hundreds of miles from nowhere, it was miserable under the best of circumstances and it was a wretched and pitiable place in January 1987."[5]

During the second Sudanese civil war (1983-2005), Wau was a garrison town for the Sudanese armed forces that were cleansing the Bahr el Ghazal of the SPLA. Wau was the scene of extensive fighting in the spring of 1998 when soldiers of the SPLA in the Bahr el Ghazal loyal to their commander Kerubino Kuanyin Bol attacked the town in an attempt of taking it from the government. Many people died. During most of the period of the second Sudanese civil war, Loyola Secondary School was used as a barracks for the government military.

Wau is in the Bahr el Ghazal region of South Sudan. Bahr el Ghazal means the rivers of the gazelles. It refers to the rivers that flow in the western part of South Sudan that forms part of the Nile Basin. Bahr el Ghazal region has an area of about 93,900 km^2. It is the least populous region in South Sudan. It shares international borders with the Sudan to the north and the Central African Republic (CAR) to the west. The Bahr el Ghazal also borders the troubled Darfur region of the Sudan.

---

[5] J. Millard Burr and Robert O. Collins. *Requiem for the Sudan: War, Drought, and Disaster Relief on the Nile* (Boulder: Westview Press, 1995), 74-75.

Wau had strong economic and social ties with Khartoum in former times. There was a train that ferried people and goods from Khartoum to Wau and back. It was a major business center with Khartoum. Many Arab traders came to Wau, and they brought with them their culture and religion. Many Arabs settled in Wau and made it their home. Wau was the most "Arabized" town in southern Sudan at the time of my arrival. This is because of its close ties with Khartoum.

The Arabic influence was still pervasive in the school system when I arrived. Other towns in South Sudan were moving away from Arabic medium of education but in Wau it seemed that people resisted the new English medium education. There was a teacher from a nearby primary school who did not know English but was asked to teach in English. He used to go for English lessons in the evening and then he would teach in English the following morning!

* * *

I was happy that I was walking in the footsteps of dedicated Jesuits who had come to Wau many years before me. I felt indebted to them and wanted to make my journey with the South Sudanese people a special gift to the people and to the Jesuits who came before me. I will write about the experiences of the Jesuits who inspired me during my stay in South Sudan as this story progresses. Their experience became an inspiration for me to radically follow in the footsteps of Christ in that challenging situation. I was not travelling alone.

Fr. Mike Lavelle, SJ who was once the superior of the Detroit Province of the Society of Jesus, on a trip to visit the

Jesuits there, described Wau town of 1981 in the following manner:

> "A few facts concerning the city of Wau: there is a center city area of ten to twelve square blocks which would have buildings of one, perhaps two stories at the most. These would be made of baked mud brick or a red stone which is found all over the area. Beyond this center city, the rest of the city spreads out in a westerly and southerly direction. It is bounded on the east by the Jur River which effectively closes off any development eastward of the city since there is only one bridge across the river. Passage over this bridge is controlled by a police sentry station. Within the center city area, there is electricity supplied by the city. However, the flow of electrical current is sporadic, depending upon the functioning of the city generators. An institution beyond the center city that wishes to have electricity would have to get a private generator, powered by gasoline or diesel fuel. The area beyond the center city is composed of mud houses, not necessarily brick, one room, no electricity, thatched roof, no plumbing or running water."[6]

Electrical power supply to the town was completely non-existent at the time of my arrival, but I could see the old non-functioning power station in one part of the town. Electricity poles could be seen throughout the town. There was no running water in the town, and people depended on water that was sold

---

[6] Report about a visit to Wau on September 12-26, 1981 by Fr. Michael J. Lavelle.

out of hand-dug wells. Many water vendors could be seen moving around the town with their donkeys.

The town of Wau had expanded at the time of my arrival, more than what Fr. Lavelle saw in 1981. I did not consider Wau a city as Fr. Lavelle named it but rather it was a town. There was a post office in the town, but it did not function, just as in the other towns of South Sudan. It seemed that the town had stretched more to the western end of Wau towards the airport and the town center was larger than the ten to twelve blocks that Fr. Lavelle saw in 1981. The police sentry on the Jur River bridge was still there during the time I lived in the town. All cars that passed over the bridge had to register with the police at the sentry post. Fr. Lavelle continued to observe that:

> "[…] the infrastructure of the city is extremely meager. The roads are atrocious. Transportation is done by truck or Land Rover or the equivalent of the Land Rover. There are very few private automobiles in the city. I saw perhaps five or six in the fourteen days I was there. There is a hospital (Wau Hospital) and a doctor. However, most Westerners in town agree that the hospital is terrible. Some Westerners indicated that they would much prefer to try to rid out a sickness or chance a long journey to Nairobi rather than use the hospital in Wau. The economy of the area is almost non-existent. Most people, it seemed to me, lived on their own garden plots which produce vegetables and a grain called *durra*. There are some livestock. One of the tribes in the area, the Dinka, are herdsmen. There

have also large herds of goats. The cattle and goats
have free run of most of the city area."[7]

The roads that I saw when I arrived fit the description of Fr. Lavelle; apart from the new part of town which had a stretch of paved road full of potholes and in a state of disrepair. Land Rovers were nonexistent in my time there. There were many Land Cruisers which most of the Church personnel and NGOs used.

There were three main hospitals in the town. Wau Teaching Hospital was a government hospital which functioned pretty well. One day, in November 2012, a man shot dead a doctor in that hospital and injured many other people because his wife died there. The hospital was subsequently closed for two weeks. There was also the Daniel Comboni Hospital, which was operated by some Religious Sisters from several missionary congregations on behalf of Catholic Diocese of Wau. This hospital was preferred by many people because it was cheap and had fairly good services. These two hospitals were in the town center.

* * *

Groundnuts were a common crop in Wau. It was the main crop in the environs of the town alongside maize, sorghum, millet which was commonly known as *durra* the grain which Fr. Lavelle mentioned in his 1981 report (see above). There were homestead industries which produced peanut butter which was a common delicacy in the town. Soup made from groundnuts

---

[7] Report about a visit to Wau on September 12-26, 1981 by Fr. Michael J. Lavelle.

was common. The homemade peanut butter was known as *tania* in Arabic. The *tania* was crushed using a small but dangerous machine which had many small blades.

The economy of Wau was booming when I arrived there in 2012 contrary to the experience of Fr. Lavelle, who arrived there in 1981. There were many foreigners in the town who engaged in several business activities. The locals too were engaged in many activities in the central bazaar known as Souk Jou. Fr. Lavelle described the bazaar in the following manner: "In the center city, the bazaar, again similar to Indian bazaars, is an area which seems to be controlled mostly by Muslim Arabs and Greek merchants."[8]

It was common to see traders from Kenya, Uganda, Sudan (from Khartoum and Darfur) and even some from as far as Egypt and Syria in the bazaar. The Arab traders were mostly identified by the turbans they had on their heads. The Greek merchants that Fr. Lavelle saw in 1981 were nowhere to be seen when I arrived in 2012. In my experience, commodities in the souks of Wau and other towns in South Sudan were very expensive, almost double the prices of commodities in other East African markets. This is because most of the commodities were imported from neighboring countries. It was also difficult to bring goods into the country because of poor infrastructure and exorbitant taxes charged on the imported goods.

Souk Jou could be considered as the lifeline of Wau. The money generated at that bazaar was enormous. One could hardly say that people in Wau live out of their gardens as observed by Fr. Lavelle in 1981. Most of the people in Wau engaged in modern business deals. Hardware shops,

---

[8] Report about a visit to Wau on September 12-26, 1981 by Fr. Michael J. Lavelle.

supermarkets, butcheries, salons and cloth shops compliment the main souk in the bustling business mini-metropolis of Wau.

Many bazaars dominated the town of Wau. Most of the businesses took place in these bazaars which were fairly well organized although most of them were covered with piles of dust. *Tukuls* and *raqubas* were found all over Wau town. There were other souks in the town. Souk Wau seemed to be the second biggest after souk Jou. Both Souk Jou and Souk Wau were part of the old town of Wau. That part of town was built during the colonial period. The buildings there were old. That part gave the town a sense of history. Some of the houses there were dilapidated due to the ravages of war and disrepair. There were other smaller souks in the town too.

Many people lived in houses that were found in the town center. If one drove through the town during evening hours, one could see people, especially men, seated under mango trees playing cards, conversing and sipping endless cups of *chai* (tea). Mango trees were common all over South Sudan, with the mango season spanning the months of March to May. It was also common to see men seated on the streets of the town smoking a concoction of tobacco in the form of steam coming from a special pipe known as *shisha*. They also played the African stone game which is known as *naqala* in Arabic or *bao* in Swahili.

Public transport was by mode of *Raksha* (see above) and motorbikes. The motorbike riders could be careless at times, and they enjoyed racing. The transport system was efficient considering the size and level of development of the town. Accidents rarely occurred although the roads were rough even in the town center.

There were also many huge horses in the town that were

used to transport heavy loads from one point to another. The horses originated from the Darfur region, and were brought to Wau by the many Darfurian merchants who could be seen in the main bazaar. It was common to see the horses galloping across the main bazaar carrying heavy loads. I never saw young horses in Wau, all of them were mature ones.

In 1981, Fr. Lavelle continued to observe that:

> "East of the Jur River, there has been an increase of sleeping sickness caused by tsetse flies. In some of river areas outside the city of Wau but within the region of Bahr el Ghazal, there has been an incidence of OV disease, a fly-caused disease that brings on blindness. Everybody, it seems, eventually gets one attack of Malaria no matter what pills you take."[9]

The OV disease described by Fr. Lavelle continued to be a problem even during my time in the town. Onchocerciasis, also known as "African River Blindness," is a filarial infection caused by the nematode *Onchocerca volvulus* (OV) that can lead to visual indisposition. The place that was worst hit by the disease was the area around Bussere River, a tributary flowing into the Jur River.

There were many incidences of malaria and typhoid, but these two diseases could easily be controlled if people slept under mosquito nets to ward off malaria carrying mosquitoes and if they ensured that the food and water that they consumed was clean. Treatment for malaria and typhoid could be sought in the hospitals in Wau town.

---

[9] Report about a visit to Wau on September 12-26, 1981 by Fr. Michael J. Lavelle.

* * *

During my stay in Wau, I noticed that many people in the town consulted witchdoctors when they experienced illnesses. Most people thought that they had been bewitched when they became ill. They would go to hospitals after the witchdoctors failed to cure them. Some of the witchdoctors knew how to administer herbs that treated their clients. Magicians were also sought to explain misfortunes that befell people. Even educated people went to the magicians and witchdoctors. These magicians and witchdoctors required payment in the form of domestic animals such as chickens and goats. It was common to find people who claimed that they had been bewitched by their neighbors or even family members because of jealously.

The most common bewitchment was known as *thogo*. It was common among the Belanda Bviri people who were the majority in the town of Wau. It involved smearing a certain magic charm on a surface where the one to be bewitched was to touch. Upon touching the charm, the victim would develop a bad swelling on the part of the body that came in contact with the charm. One had to go to another witchdoctor who would undo the effects of the charm after a lot of excruciating pain. Others had to undergo mini-surgeries in Wau town to get rid of *thogo*.

The most feared witches seemed to be from the Azande ethnic group who originally came from the Western Equatoria region of South Sudan. Wau town had a significant number of the Azande people who had migrated into the area. It was common to hear that a Zande person had been the cause of misfortune to a person of another ethnic group. The Azande people in Wau were treated with much suspicion. The Azande do not have the concept of bad luck; everything must have a cause. There is nothing accidental in the Azande mentality. Withcraft causes all misfortunes among the Azande. *Witchcraft, Oracles, and Magic Among the Azande* is an in-depth study of witchcraft among the Azande by E.E Evans-Pritchard.[10] In it, he outlines the basic processes that take place during bewitchment among the Azande. One fascinating thing about this is that among the Azande, one can be a witch without his or her knowledge.

One day, one of my students at Loyola Secondary School explained to me his misfortune. He had developed a stomach ailment after drinking water given to him by an old Azande woman who was known to be a witch or had witchcraft tendencies. The student had sought medical attention in several hospitals in Wau, but the doctors told him that he was not sick in any way. The student was advised by his relatives to consult a famous Azande medium in a nearby village. This medium was good at performing oracles which solved people's problems. The medium listened to the whole story carefully. He then began drawing some strange diagrams on the ground while saying in the Zande language, "You earth: you have to tell us; is this problem from the victim's mother or the father?" After a series of magical performances, the medium concluded that the illness was from the mother and he prescribed a concoction which the student had to drink immediately. The student did not want to drink the concoction because it was too bitter. He held it in his mouth and threw it out afterwards. He paid the medium for the services rendered before he left the

---

[10] See E. E. Evans-Pritchard, *Witchcraft, Oracles, and Magic Among the Azande* (Oxford: Oxford University Press, 1976).

place. The medium told the student to return the following day for more treatment with a black chicken and a lamb. The student was traumatized by the whole affair and came to me for advice. He did not go back to the Azande medium.

I was not so sure what to do with witchcraft while I lived in Wau. When students brought to me a witchcraft case, such as the one narrated above, I would always listen to the story in a non- judgmental way as much as I could, and then I tried to respond to the person in light of the Christian faith tradition. Sometimes I was successful in reassuring the person, which is what most of them needed, sometimes I was not. When I failed, I tried not to be too hard on myself but to let God be in control. I learned that I was not called to solve problems but rather to accompany people by listening, reassuring and by being a loving presence and to leave the rest to God.

* * *

During my stay in Wau, in March and April, the town experienced strong dusty winds from the north. It was a kind of sand storm coming from Khartoum. These winds occurred towards the end of the dry season. The winds were known as the *haboob*. It was said that the *haboob* that was experienced in Wau was not as strong as the ones that occurred in Khartoum, which is in the Sahara Desert and, thus, experiences the real sand storms. The *haboob* used to destroy many semi-permanent houses in Wau, just before the rainy season began.

Wau was a cosmopolitan town when I arrived there in 2012. It was composed of people from different ethnic affiliations. The people of Wau were fond of naming their suburbs with the word *shedid* (little) to recreate a home away from their original home. For example, the people of Rumbek shedid (little Rumbek) suburb were mostly Dinka from Rumbek, and the residents of Bagari shedid (little Bagari) were the Belanda Bviri people originating from the village of Bagari, which was a few miles out of Wau.

The town of Wau was polarized with the Dinka and the "Jur" (Luo) people being against the members of the "Fertit" group. The Fertit are what Collins and Burr described above as a group of "Sudanic cultivators" crushed between the Dinka people coming from the north of Wau and the Azande people originating from the south of the town in the Equatoria region. The Dinka and the "Jur" are of similar complexion and cultural backgrounds.

In my experience, the central bazaar, souk Jou, seemed to be the dividing line between the Dinka and the non-Dinka areas of Wau town. Loyola Secondary School was located in the non-Dinka area. Most of the jobs in the town of Wau had been taken up by the Dinka, and this made the other groups feel alienated.

Many northern Sudanese Arab traders, known as Jelaba, also lived in Wau and thus their street was known as Hai Jelaba. The Jelaba seemed to be living happily in Wau even though some of their compatriots moved back to Khartoum after the separation of South Sudan from Sudan in 2011. The Jelaba had a distinct kind of dress: they wore long Islamic robes which were known as *jelabia*. The jelabia were of a variety of colors. Many Christians people had adopted this dress in the town.

The Jelaba were asked to choose between the two countries in 2011, and some of them opted for South Sudan. They enjoyed citizenship rights just like any other South Sudanese, although they were still considered "different" by the local people. The categorization of streets and suburbs by ethnic names polarized the town, and ethnic violence occurred periodically.

The students at Loyola Secondary School came from the above diverse groups, although a large percentage of them were Belanda Bviri, who originated from the little village of Bagari, which is a few kilometers northwest of Loyola. There was fear that Dinka people would not send their children to study at Loyola because it was located in a Balanda Bviri area. There was a considerable amount of tension between the Dinka and the Belanda Bviri, but this did not stop Dinka students from coming to Loyola. There were harmonious relationships among the students from the different ethnic affiliations during my time at Loyola. The school situation instilled in them the value of respecting each other's ethnic identities. It was a joy to see all the cultures that were represented in the town. I used to enjoy a weekly stroll through the main bazaar looking at the people going on with their lives in their diverse and simple ways. The diversity of food, clothing styles, and language was fascinating to experience.

* * *

The town of Wau had an airport which was not working when I arrived there because it was under repair. An airplane had crashed on the rough runway a few months before, and that forced the government to build a proper runway. The airport was closed for about one year and was renovated with the help of the Chinese-United Nations Mission in South Sudan (UNMISS). The renovated airport had a modern paved runway. Nevertheless, the immigration offices, and the waiting lounge were in disrepair. The waiting lounge was poorly built with very low ceiling and poor ventilation. To sit there could be compared to sitting in an oven because of the high temperatures! There was a smallish immigration room near the waiting lounge in which all international people arriving in Wau were summoned into for questioning. The airport did not receive international flights.

At the time of my departure from Wau, frequent airplanes were flying out of Wau Airport to Juba although they were unpredictable. One had to strategize how to get out of Wau for weeks before the actual departure. Flights were always fully booked and in some cases overbooked. It was common for people to go to the airport only to return home because the flight was overbooked or cancelled.

The World Food Program (WFP) managed United Nations Humanitarian Air Service (UNHAS) flights seemed to be the most reliable. However, getting a seat on that flight involved a lot of frustrating bureaucracies. Apart from obtaining a ticket, one needed a letter of introduction or an identification card from the organization that one worked with in order to get onboard. People who used the UNHAS flight had to be workers of organizations accredited by UNHAS. For the case of the Jesuits in Wau, the Diocese of Wau was not accredited to UNHAS but Diocese of Rumbek (DOR) was, and so we got seats on the UNHAS flights through our cordial relationship with DOR. It took about a week to make a booking with the UNHAS people, but one was sure that he or she would travel to wherever they wanted in South Sudan.

The UNHAS flights in South Sudan cater for the need for available transport in times of natural disaster or conflict which is crucial. In conflict situations, communities can quickly become displaced and left without proper access to food, water, and shelter. A rapid response can save lives, and air transport is often the only way to move fast enough. WFP/UNHAS provide air transportation for emergency response on the front lines of hunger and other conflict related emergencies. WFP/UNHAS provides efficient, safe and reliable air transport services to over seven hundred humanitarian organizations operating around the world.[11] The Catholic Church operating in conflict and disaster zones such as in South Sudan qualifies as a humanitarian agency that can use this service.

Getting out of Wau was one thing; getting back to Wau from Juba was another. One could spend up to five days in Juba before getting a ticket back to Wau. Sometimes the planes were overbooked, and people would be told to wait for another plane which would be available in two or three days. Travelling in South Sudan taught me a lot about relying on divine providence. A person was never sure if he or she was going to travel until he or she was airborne.

Beyond Wau airport was an area known as Bil Pham. That was a place where the returnees from Khartoum, who came back after the separation of South Sudan from Sudan took place, were settled. The camp was also known as Khartoum Shedid, little Khartoum. It was a huge area that had many semi-permanent houses. This resettlement camp was similar to the one found in Rumbek. Life there was rough and tough but the people seemed happy.

---

[11] See http://www.wfp.org/logistics/aviation/unhas-current-operations.

* * *

The Catholic cathedral church in Wau is an enormous building, imposing if you like. It was about a kilometer from the main bazaar, souk Jou. It dominated, as it were, towered above the town of Wau. In former times, the size of this cathedral was a source of consternation and anger to the Islamic government in Khartoum. It was built by the Comboni Missionaries who brought the Catholic Church to Wau at the beginning of the 20th century. It was a work of art, built of burnt bricks and towering up to 200 feet, perhaps even more. It was built in the form of the Roman Cathedrals found in Italy. On the inside, there were frescos of various saints and stained-glass windows. I was surprised to see such a magnificent building in the midst of poverty and underdevelopment. At the time of my arrival in Wau, the magnificent church needed to be repaired and painted because the amount of dust that had accumulated on the building over the years.

The Comboni Missionaries have evangelized the Wau area since the beginning of the 20th century. Even after over 100 years of evangelization, the Church in Wau and South Sudan, in general, was still dependent on missionaries. The Church had not grown out of the missionary stage of its development. This was mainly because of the effects of more than a century of injustice and marginalization caused by wars and exploitation of the south of Sudan by Islamic government in Khartoum.

The Mission compound and the Cathedral complex are separated by the Raga Road which heads west out of the town and goes as far as Central African Republic. The mission compound was under the custody of the Bishop of Wau, Rudolf

Deng Majak when I arrived in Wau in 2012. The Comboni Missionaries priests had moved out of it and established their house in another part of the town where they were running a vibrant parish. In the Mission compound, there was the diocesan radio known as Radio Voice of Hope, the parish house, Pastoral Liturgical and Catechetical Coordination Center (PALICA) and three convents for Religious Sisters who worked around Wau (Comboni, Franciscan, and Nazareth). There was also a small old church which was the cathedral before the huge and complex building across the Raga road was built. The small church was used as a private chapel for the diocesan staff and members of the various religious congregations of priests and nuns who worked in Wau.

Bishop Deng Majak was a Dinka from Warap region of South Sudan; from the Rek clan of the Dinka. He had been the apostolic administrator of the Diocese from 1991 to 1996 when he was consecrated Bishop of Wau. His predecessor in the episcopate of Wau was Bishop Joseph Bilal Nyekindi, who in 1981 when he became Bishop of Wau, invited the Jesuits to start Loyola Secondary School. Upon his retirement in 1991, Bishop Nyekindi went to work with the physically challenged people in the troubled region of Abyei where he died in 1996.

Bishop Majak was an approachable and lovely man with a broad smile who had his door always open to anyone who wanted to see him for a chat. He could be seen on different occasions chatting freely with some merchants in the streets near the Mission compound during evening hours. He was a man of the people. Bishop Majak died in March 2017 after a long illness. He inspired me to be a person of faith, hope, and love for God and God's people.

On a hill overlooking the cathedral, there was a mosque

with two tower-like pillars which seemed to have been in competition with the massive Catholic cathedral which was down the hill. Judging from its appearance, the mosque in Wau was a fairly recent spectacle in the town. The number of Muslims in Wau was small compared to the Catholic Christians.

During my time there, I had a sense that most of the people in Wau were Roman Catholics. Pentecostal churches could be found but in a rather small scale. Catholicism and Islam seemed to be the most dominant forms of religion. A few Loyola Secondary School students who were Muslims would get permission to go for mosque prayers every Friday. A sizeable population of Wau practiced African Traditional Religions (ATR). Religious harmony was a hallmark of the people in Wau; I never heard a story of religious violence during my time there.

* * *

The most common mode of transmitting information in Wau during my time there was by word of mouth. Rumors abounded in the town, and one would find different versions of the same story circulating. The culture in Wau was mainly an oral one, where stories were given precedence over facts. It was common to see people congregated around a storyteller who in most cases told embellished stories about what was happening in the town.

Notwithstanding the above, important information from the regional government in the town was disseminated by public announcements over a loudspeaker. A car would move around, and a pre-recorded announcement would be played over and over in the Arabic language. There was a man who was designated to do that job, and his voice was the "standard" announcing voice in Wau. He was, as it were, the mouthpiece of the town. Arabic music punctuated the announcements. The announcements were disseminated in this way mainly at night when people were in their houses. The most common announcement when I lived and worked in Wau was that the government had declared the following day as a public holiday, because of various reasons. These holidays caused a lot of disruption in schools and other public institutions in the town. Even though these announcements were made, different interpretations were given by a variety of people about what was announced. One could get as many as five interpretations of what was announced over the loudspeaker the night before.

No national newspaper was distributed in the town. There was neither a national radio nor a television network that broadcasted news in the town. There was only one community radio station in Wau that was run by the Catholic Church. Other towns in South Sudan such as Tonj, Rumbek, and Juba had such community radios operated by the Catholic Church. The only radio station that had a nationwide coverage was Radio *Miraya,* which was run by the United Nations.

Chapter Four

The Will to Help Others

"The purpose of human life is to serve, and to show compassion and the will to help others."

Albert Schweitzer

In life, God sends people into other people's lives to inspire them. These are people whose extraordinary courage and zeal for the greater glory of God are unshakeable. They believe that the world can be a better place if only people can focus on selfless service especially for the poor and the dispossessed. Such people are altruistic and are determined to follow what they consider to be right. Their main motive is to serve others compassionately. I met one such person on the day of my arrival in Wau in 2012: Fr Richard Cherry, SJ.

Fr. Cherry, was one of the pioneers of Loyola Secondary School. He was an American from Toledo, OH, who formerly belonged to the then Detroit Province of the Society of Jesus before he became a missionary in India. He arrived in Wau in 1985 after serving as a missionary for many years in Patna, India, where he had taught physics at a high school. He was ordained a priest in Patna and became a member of that Jesuit

Province. He later moved to the Eastern Africa Province of the Society of Jesus.

Fr. Cherry stayed at Loyola Secondary School in 1987, when the school was closed because of the second Sudanese civil war which began in May 1983. His job was that of a sentry: to guard the school and ensure it was not destroyed by the Khartoum soldiers who occupied the buildings. The school had become a military garrison just less than four years after its official opening. It was strategically located on a 60 feet elevation (*Jebel Kheir* or the Hill of Luck in Arabic) overlooking the town of Wau and thus the military people found it an idea spot for launching their attacks against the rebels. He was treated roughly by the soldiers one December night in 1987. He wrote of that experience in this way:

> "Shortly after I had finished my midnight Mass on Christmas Eve, the soldiers were pounding on the front gate which was locked. I went out to see what they wanted only to find about five or six of them with their weapons waiting to escort me to the commander's room. There, my hands were tied behind my back (in such a way, however, as to be able easily to extricate myself) and told to sit on the verandah. There was no word from the commander, who didn't directly meet me though he was around and most certainly aware of what was happening because there was muttering about no water. I was then tied loosely to a post outside the commander's room. I remained there throughout the night though I removed my hands from the rope and lay back in a more comfortable position to rest and pray. About

> 5:00 am the commander arose and at 5:30 am told one of the soldiers to free me. So, I gave them back their rope and went to my room to sleep."[12]

The above incident illustrates how courageous and fearless Fr. Charry was in his quest to be an agent of good in a very difficult situation. He was the only Jesuit living in Wau at the end of the 1980s at the height of the civil war. Many people feared for his life, but he was convinced that that was where God wanted him to be at that time.

Fr. Cherry left Wau in 1991 after being ordered to leave the town by the military. The military people who were controlling Loyola had had enough of him! He then went to Adjumani in northern Uganda where he lived and worked with Sudanese refugees until 1995. At that time, he was working with the Jesuit Refugee Service (JRS). Afterwards, he joined the faculty of the newly founded Jesuit School Loyola High School Dar es Salaam, Tanzania. He had fallen in love with the Sudan and was ready to come back after the signing of the Comprehensive Peace Agreement (CPA) in 2005. Nostalgia for Wau never left him until the end.

Fr. Cherry came back to Wau in 2005, to begin again a mission of spreading hope after many years of absence. He died on April 3, 2013, in the United States of America. Fr. Cherry was a meticulous man in everything that he did. He never settled for mediocrity. He was a physics teacher, a subject he loved through and through. His room at the Jesuit Community in Wau was like a laboratory with all kinds of equipment properly stored in their respective shelves and marked. He was a silent man and would do his work quietly.

---

[12] Letter to Fr. Paul Besanceney by Fr. Richard Cherry, SJ on January 18, 1988.

Fr. Cherry welcomed me to Wau on the evening of my arrival and asked if I was visiting or had come to stay whereupon I told him that I had come to stay. He was a man with a sense of humor. His first advice to the Jesuits who came to Wau was, "if you have doubts about the water in Wau, you better try a beer; with that, you are sure that it is clean"!

* * *

A short narrative about the founding of Loyola Secondary School is necessary at this point since this narrative revolves around that school.[13] Fr. Paul H. Besanceney, SJ, and Br. Joseph A. Shubitowski, SJ both members of the Detroit Province of the Society of Jesus, left the United States for Sudan in July 1980. They were both sent to work at St. Paul's Major Seminary, which at that time was located in Bussere village, seven miles southeast of the town of Wau. Fr. Michael J. Lavelle, SJ, superior of the Detroit Province from 1977-1983, visited Fr. Besanceney and Br. Shubitowski in Bussere in September 1981.

During that visit, the Bishop of the Catholic Diocese of Wau, Joseph Bilal Nyekindi approached Fr. Lavelle and through him asked the Society of Jesus to begin a Catholic secondary school in the town of Wau. The Bishop, Br. Shubitowski, and Fr. Lavelle spent time together, looking for a favorable location for the new school. They agreed on a twenty-five-acre parcel of property, a few acres of which had an attractive sixty-foot elevation. This site, a little beyond the edge of Wau town and about three miles southwest of the cathedral

---

[13] For the story of the founding of Loyola Secondary School, Wau, I rely on the information in the chronicle written by Fr. Norman Dickson, SJ on July 13, 1988.

of Wau and a mile past the University of Bahr el Ghazal, turned out to be the place where Loyola was built. Fr. Lavelle left Wau on September 26, 1981, not guaranteeing anything to the Bishop, but certainly promising that he would take up the matter with both his consulters and the Detroit Province membership.[14]

Sometime in January 1982, during a meeting of Detroit Province of the Society of Jesus representatives at Colombiere College in Clarkston, Michigan, the proposal of Bishop Nyekindi was discussed and examined. Fr. Besanceney and Br. Shubitowski were both present at this meeting. After this and further consultation, Fr. Lavelle decided to go ahead with the project. He wrote to Rome for approval, and he wrote to the membership of both the Detroit and other U.S Provinces, asking for volunteers for this mission work.

In a letter written at Rome on July 2, 1982, Fr. Paolo Dezza, SJ who was at the time Delegate Superior General of the Society of Jesus, approved Fr. Lavelle's proposal to begin the school in Wau. To Fr. Lavelle's invitation for volunteers, six Jesuits responded. On May 21, 1982, Fr. Lavelle met with Fr. Dickson at Walsh Jesuit High School in Cuyahoga Falls, Ohio. He informed Fr. Dickson that he was accepted for the mission and that he was in charge of the project. Fr. Dickson was told to get in touch immediately with the other volunteers, selecting those he thought could help get the job done.

Thus, the initial team for the project was in place: Fr. Norman Dickson, director of the proposed school, who would leave for Sudan by the end of the summer of 1982; Fr. Robert Dietrich, Fr. Larry Belt and Scholastic Stephen Gelinas (from the Maryland Province), were designated as teachers and they

---

[14] Report about a visit to Wau on September 12-26, 1981 by Fr. Michael J. Lavelle.

would leave for Sudan at different times in 1983; Fr. Jerry Odbert, also a teacher, who would join others in 1984.

Before Fr. Dickson left the United States of America on September 20, 1982, the team members, except Scholastic Gelinas, met two times to discuss their future work. The first meeting was held at the University of Detroit on June 10, 1982; the second meeting was held at St. Ignatius High School, Cleveland, Ohio on July 2 and 3, 1982.

In a letter written in Wau on July 5, 1982, Br. Shubitowski informed Fr. Dickson that he had acquired from the local government the property site agreed upon the previous year. Br. Shubitowski also stated that for legal purposes he had to come up with a name for the school. The name he selected was Loyola Secondary School.

* * *

Six Jesuits were working in Wau at the time of my arrival there. They were all working hard amidst the challenges they were facing in that mission. The lifestyle was modest. The food prepared in the community was relatively good considering that it was difficult to find a variety of food items in the markets of Wau town.

The Jesuit Community House was very homely. If one compared it with the households found in Wau, the Jesuit house could be considered to be of very high quality. It had been built in 1982 and was renovated after the second Sudanese civil war in 2006. The rooms were simple, well-built with good ventilation. There were fine mesh wires on the windows that prevented insects such as mosquitoes from coming in. I used to leave the windows open day and night because the rooms were so hot.

The house was officially dedicated in 1984. Fr. Norman Dickson wrote the following in his chronicle about the dedication of the house:

> "On July 31, 1984, the feast of St. Ignatius, about 35 local and foreign priests and religious joined the Loyola community for the dedication of its new residence. Bishop Nyekindi was the principal celebrant for the evening liturgy. After the Mass the guests enjoyed a tasty dinner expertly prepared by Fr. Jerry Odbert, SJ with assistance from Fr. Larry Belt, SJ."[15]

There was also a garage with two generators which supplied us with power during the night. During the daytime, we used solar power. The solar batteries were worn out and, thus, they could not sustain us at night. Hence, we needed generator power for the night. We kept a stock of diesel in that garage. To have a stock of diesel was important because we sometimes had a shortage of fuel in Wau. One time there was no fuel anywhere in Wau town for a whole month.

The generators pumped water from a water well into a 4500-liters tank. The water tank was made by Br. Shubitowski in 1982. He assembled the tank in the village of Bussere, where the Jesuits were living and teaching at St. Paul's Major Seminary. Br. Shubitowski then brought the tank up to the Loyola hill after he completed its construction.

---

[15] Norman Dickson, *Loyola Secondary School, Sudan: A Chronicle*, 20.

During my time in Wau, some strange animals used to sneak into this tank especially during the dry season to get water, and some would drown in there. Therefore, it was common to have a foul smell in the water, and that was an indication that a creature had drowned in the tank. Someone had to climb in there to do some cleaning. This tank also provided water for the school.

Water remained a big problem for the people of Wau most of whom did not have water wells. The UN had drilled three water wells in the Loyola compound for the local people around the school so that they could have clean water. However, the hand pumps were always destroyed by chidren who played there. It was common to see water vendors carrying water in small tanks drawn by donkeys. The water from these vendors was mostly likely contaminated. Cases of typhoid and other communicable diseases caused by contaminated water were rampant in Wau. This situation was made worse by the lack of toilet facilities in the area.

One evening during an informal conversation, a Jesuit advised me not to shake hands with the students and the teachers. This was because there was a culture common in Wau of not using toilet paper after visiting the toilet. People would rather use water to clean up after a toilet visit. I did not pay attention to that because I felt that that would have been too alienating to the people. Instead, I was careful to wash my hands with soap before meals. Our students were also relatively clean, and they maintained good standards of hygiene.

The UN presence was obvious from the time of my arrival in South Sudan. The UN people were trying to help the South Sudanese people to build the new country from scratch. Apart from peace keeping initiatives, the UN worked with schools such as Loyola Secondary School and other institutions in order to educate the people. In Wau, there were several UN battalions from all over the world. They had their camp on the western end of Wau town near Wau Airport. I was impressed by the humanitarian work they did. The Chinese UN has a nice hospital that served the local people in addition to other humanitarian work they did around Wau.

* * *

One evening, during those early days, a Jesuit took me around Loyola Secondary School to see what was there. There were three major buildings which constituted the school. My first impression was that it was a small school. The buildings were modest. There was no electricity in the school. If one wanted to use a computer, one had to charge it at the Jesuit community and then bring it over to the school. All the examinations were duplicated in the Jesuit community. The school's water supply came from the water tank at the Jesuit community.

At the time of my arrival at Loyola Secondary School, extensive plans had been made to modernize the school in order to bring it to the level of the other Jesuit schools in Eastern Africa. A series of meetings were held in October 2008 to discuss the expansion of the school. A master plan was put together with the help of a Canadian architect who spent six weeks in Wau, getting actual measurements through ground survey from the site of the proposed buildings. The master plan that resulted was extensive, and it was envisioned that it would be carried out in at least four phases. The first phase of the plan, which was aimed at building six new classrooms, was completed when I arrived in Wau in 2012. Difficulties to build the other parts of the school will be narrated later in this narrative.

The grounds around the school compound were full of bullet cartridges. More and more of these cartridges would get exposed especially after heavy rains. No matter how much we collected them, more cartridges were exposed. This is because the old buildings in the school were used as a military garrison. A Jesuit showed me some live bullets that he had collected in the school compound over the years. There were also landmines in the school compound, but they were all removed before the reopening of the school took place in 2008. There was a remnant of a missile launcher just outside the old classes on the eastern part of the school compound. Some Jesuits claimed that that was a sign that the soldiers would return to occupy the school. That was an unfounded fear because, after the peace agreement of 2005, circumstances changed in ways that it would be unthinkable for one to expect that a school in South Sudan could be turned into a military barracks again. Close to the old classrooms, there were remnants of the trenches which the soldiers used during the war.

There was a graveyard in one corner of the school. The graves there, most likely, belonged to the people who had died during the second Sudanese civil war (1983-2005). These graves were later fenced out of the school's property. There were other graves scattered around the school which could not be fenced out. The presence of these graves was a constant reminder of the ravages of the war. Some people around Jebel Kheir believed that the spirits of the dead buried in and around the school were not happy, and these spirits were causing misfortune to the people there and to the school community.

There was a teacher's quarter in the school. It had four

rooms, a kitchen, and a sitting room. It lacked electricity and water. The house needed to be furnished with basic amenities. There were two teachers (Ugandan and Kenyan) who lived in that house in 2012.

The original idea when the reopening of the school occurred in 2008 was to have several teacher's quarters in the school compound where teachers from outside South Sudan could come and live on a permanent basis. This vision could have helped solve the problem of lack of teachers at Loyola Secondary School. South Sudan has very few trained teachers. Even those teachers who have been trained would prefer to do other well-paying jobs rather than teach in schools.

* * *

At the time of my arrival at Loyola Secondary School, the students seemed to be a happy folk even though most of them were born during the civil war. The resilience they showed was spectacular. After all the trauma, they still could smile and radiate joy. I was happy to be there to share my life with them.

Most of the students there had malleable personalities and were ready, even excited, to learn. This gave me a lot of hope for a bright future for South Sudan. One interesting phenomenon that I quickly noted was that there was a student who acted as a school translator. He had to translate what was being said in English into Arabic during the school assembly times. He was nicknamed, the "general school translator." The translation was done because some new students did not understand English because they came from Arabic medium primary schools.

I felt so happy to be among the young people at Loyola Secondary School. They radiated a lot of joy, and I felt that the future of the country was going to be bright. In the midst of the depravation, poverty, the many other challenges they were facing, and the years of war, I could not but marvel at how they continued to keep hope alive. They taught me to keep trusting in the slow work of God.

I noticed, just on my arrival, that the school was not the usual schools I had seen elsewhere in Africa. The infrastructure was meager; the students were much older, the whole situation seemed new to me. Later, I was told that what I was witnessing was called "Emergency Education" in a post-war situation. This kind of education responds to the needs of post-war communities in an adaptable way. The little resources that are available to the post-war communities are used creatively to produce positive outcomes. The Jesuits were in the process of making the school a normal one, but the process had a lot of logistical challenges.

Some few students, at the time of my arrival at Loyola Secondary School, were over thirty years old. The 21 years of civil war had delayed the education of many people, and some of them were determined to get an education no matter how old they were. One such student was the village elder of the area where Loyola was located.

The school was staffed by part time teachers. The only full-time staff were the Jesuits. In such circumstances, it was difficult to inculcate values to the students because the teachers did not feel responsible for character formation of the students. They would rather teach their lessons and disappear from the school as early as they could.

* * *

The high school classes in Wau were known as seniors. They ranged from senior one up to senior three. At Loyola and a few other schools in Wau, there was also a preparatory class, that ran for one year, which aimed at helping students improve their English proficiency before joining senior one. This is because most students who joined Loyola were from primary schools that taught in Arabic. School time at Loyola was from 7:30 a.m. to 3:20 p.m., with the main break time at 10:00 a.m. and another one at 12:45 p.m. Most of the students carried packed food from home, but it seemed to me that the food they brought was not always enough.

At the 10:00 a.m. break, the students would have their breakfast which they called *foutur*. *Foutur* was a meal that served as both breakfast and lunch. *Foutur* was a custom of the people all over Wau. One interesting thing was that at around the time of *foutur*, one would see some primary school students carrying their chairs (most primary schools did not have chairs, and so pupils had to bring chairs from home) and going back to their homes about one and a half hours after they had headed towards school. The school day had ended! Some of these students would go to Wau town to roam. It was common to see some primary school students loitering around Loyola instead of going to their respective schools.

The primary schools (grade schools) in Wau were mostly in bad conditions. There was a severe lack of teachers, discipline levels were a bare minimum, and noisemaking was the order of the day in those schools. One nearby primary school had only two teachers: the headmaster and his deputy who would teach about 400 students in turns for the whole day.

Because of the poor primary school conditions, some students who came to Loyola for their secondary school education were indiscipline and very difficult to educate. Nevertheless, the primary schools that were managed by the Catholic church fared much better; they produced better quality of students. Most of the student who came to join Loyola had excellent primary school examinations result, an average of about 70%. On inquiring about how this could be possible given the nature of the primary schools, I was told that most of these students participated in cheating in their examinations.

The curriculum followed at Loyola at the time of my arrival would lead to a graduate to get the Sudan Secondary School Certificate. Everything was controlled in Khartoum, Sudan although South Sudan became independent in July 2011. All the textbooks were in Arabic, but we had textbooks translated from Arabic to English produced by the Comboni College Khartoum (CCK). CCK had a long history in educating Sudanese people. It was established in 1955, a year before the independence of the Sudan from the Anglo-Egyptian rulers, by the Comboni Missionaries. CCK served as a haven for the Jesuits when the first arrived in Khartoum in the 1970s and 1980s.

In 2012, most schools in South Sudan were still following the Khartoum syllabus because the new South Sudan syllabus had been difficult to implement due to of lack of resources to produce books and also lack of proper personnel who would implement this syllabus.

Some of the contents of the syllabus were, according to me, beyond the scope of the students. There were seventeen subjects taught in the school: English, Special Arabic, Chemistry, Physics, Biology, Basic Mathematics, Additional

Mathematics, History, Geography, Agriculture, Family Science, Commercial Science, Religion, Military Science, Computer Science, Fine Art and Engineering Science. Senior one and two classes were expected to take at least sixteen subjects. This was too much for the students! It was not worthwhile to have such a demanding curriculum. I was shocked by this situation. It was believed that the Khartoum government had deliberately made the education system complicated in the South so that the non-Arabs there could be discouraged from getting an education.

Part of this curriculum was designed for Islamic schools in the Sudan. For example, the history that was taught was mostly an Islamic history geared toward brainwashing the students so that they could think that the Arabs were superior to the black southerners. The content of the subject Military Science was mostly about the glorification of the military prowess of the Arabs throughout history. Fr. Bernard Mallia, SJ was furious that a Jesuit school, in a predominantly Christian country, could allow such a disgraceful subject to be taught.

Some of the content taught in the sciences were of university level. I taught biology in senior one when I first arrived at the school, and I was shocked that parts of the syllabus was what I had learnt when I was a freshman at a Kenyan university. Most of the students found this very difficult.

Getting teachers for subjects such as Geography and Arabic was difficult. The Arabic teachers we had in the school did not speak English. Thus, it was hard to follow up what they were doing in the classes because the Jesuits, who controlled the school, did not speak, read or write Arabic well.

One time, an Arabic examination had its title: بِسْمِ اللهِ

بِسْمِ اللهِ الرَّحْمٰنِ الرَّحِيْمِ - *Bismillah-ir-Rahman-ir-Rahim* (In the Name of Allah, the Most Gracious, the Most Merciful) written in the Arabic alphabet. I was taken aback when I learned about that. I wondered how learning Arabic grammar was connected with Islamic religion. This was a sign of how deep the "Islamization" of the Christian south by the Muslim north had been. This was not okay because we were not proselytizing in the school but rather we, were trying to form responsible citizens.

Fr. Richard Cherry, SJ observed that just a few students passed the Sudan School Certificate Examination in the 1980s because the exams were so difficult. Some schools recorded 100% failure. The pass rate at the time of my arrival was above 60%, but most of the students passed the exam after copying from one another or from books. Cheating in exams was a common occurance, and we had to work hard to eradicate that vice. The students learned to cheat in examinations in their primary schools and by the time they joined secondary schools they found it hard to change. Nonetheless, some of the students worked very hard and could perform very well even with the difficult content; without cheating.

There was a poor reading culture in the school when I arrived. Reading was like a punishment to the students. The culture in Wau was an oral one and, thus, speaking was considered more valuable than reading. The library at the school was used as a venue for punishing students. It was common to see teachers sending students to the library for a few hours after they have made mistakes as a form of punishment! To be silent for a few hours was unbearable for some students.

There were many logistical challenges that Loyola faced.

For example, it was very difficult to duplicate examinations at Loyola. Sometimes the photocopiers would break down and would need special repair which was not available in Wau. One time, as we were preparing to give examinations to our students, our duplicating machines developed mechanical problems. We then decided to write the examinations on the classroom black boards. At the end of the first day of writing the examinations on the boards, I decided that I was not going to do that again because it was a nerve-wracking experience.

At the time of my arrival, there were other secondary schools in Wau. John Paul II Secondary School was the diocesan school. The standard of education there was fair. Standard Secondary School was found in a suburb known as Hai Dinka. It was a privately owned school of poor quality. The owner of the school admitted anyone who could pay school fees. There were several other secondary schools which had poor quality of education. Loyola was considered the best school in Wau and many students wanted to join the school but could not make it because they could not afford to pay the 200 US dollars (800 SSP) school fees or they could not get the required entry mark.

Chapter Five

Taking One Day at a Time

"Not all of us do great things. But we can do small things with Great love."

Mother Teresa of Calcutta

If there is one virtue that the Jesuits who worked in the Sudan and South Sudan excelled in, it is love. These were men who sacrificed their lives in order to share with people who needed their help and companionship. I had a privilege to meet such a Jesuit in the person of the illustrious Jesuit Fr. Michael Schultheis, SJ. He was an American Jesuit from the Oregon Province of the Society of Jesus. He came to Wau during the early days of my stay there, and he inspired me to give the best I could to the people of South Sudan. His life is full of hope and joy. At that time, he was the Vice Chancellor of the Catholic University of South Sudan (CUoSS). I remembered him from a talk I had heard many years before entitled *Five Great Jesuits*. The speaker at that talk included Fr. Schultheis in his list of five great Jesuits.

Fr. Schultheis was an iconic Jesuit in the area of higher education in Africa. He taught at Makerere University in

Kampala, Uganda from 1970 to 1973. He also taught at the University of Dar es Salaam, Tanzania in the 1980s. Before coming to help out to start CUoSS he had facilitated the beginnings of Catholic Universities in Mozambique and Ghana. He came into Sudan to begin the new University in 2007.

He had worked with the Jesuit Refugee Service (JRS) in Mozambique and Angola. He became the director of JRS Africa from 1988 to 1992 and was based in Nairobi. He worked extensively in the Eastern Africa region to alleviate the suffering of the refugees at that time.

Fr. Schultheis started CUoSS out of nothing. It was said that he had a gift of starting things out on nothing! The Catholic University in Juba was housed in an old building. Fr. Schultheis' office served as his bedroom as well. The books in the University library were a collection that Fr. Schultheis had collected from around the world over the years.

The campus in Wau, which offered Agricultural courses, was established in a former convent of the Nazareth Sisters which was used during the war as a barracks. The buildings were old, and no newcomer could have thought that there was a university there. In November 2010, the *National Catholic Reporter* (NCR) reported the following about the University:

> "The faculty of arts and social sciences was launched in 2008 in Juba, capital of the southern region. Already, 250 students are enrolled. In 2009 a second faculty of agricultural and environmental sciences opened with some 50 students in Wau, capital of Bahr el Ghazal region. A third faculty of engineering sciences is planned for next year. "The Catholic University of Sudan as a national institution is a

dream long deferred," said its vice chancellor, Jesuit Fr. Michael Schultheis. He said the Sudan Catholic Bishops' Conference had wanted a Catholic university since Sudan gained independence from Britain in 1956. In 1983 Sudan's then President Gaafar Nimeiri spoke to Pope John Paul II about it when he visited Rome. But the initiative was soon scrapped when Nimeiri and his military government, in an effort to win support among the northern elites, applied Sharia law nationwide and tried to impose the Arabic language and Islam on the south which was a largely non-Arab, non-Muslim region. Protests by southern Sudanese sparked a return to civil war, which killed an estimated 2.5 million southerners and displaced 4.5 million."[16]

This University was the brainchild of the Sudan Catholic Bishops' Conference (SCBC). Prompted by the canonization of Bishop Daniele Comboni, the beloved Sudanese Saint and the first Bishop of the Sudan; the Holy Father John Paul II encouraged the Sudanese Bishops to establish a Catholic University in 2003. The *National Catholic Reporter* summarized the vision of the SCBC about the University in the following manner:

> "The bishops view the new university as the centerpiece of their plans to help Sudan recover from decades of violence, famine and the mass

---

[16] Lefevere Patricia, "Catholic university launches in Sudan" *National Catholic Reporter*, November 11, 2010. http://ncronline.org/news/global/catholic-university-launches-sudan.

displacement of people, Schultheis told NCR in an e-mail interview. The bishops recognize that the church is called to assist at every level in building the new Sudan. They view it as a place to train personnel with the skills and expertise to manage and provide the basic services the nation desperately needs, he said. The founding of the university comes at a historic moment as the nation prepares for a critical referendum in 2011 to decide if Sudan stays united or becomes two countries. "Sentiment in the South seems to be overwhelmingly for independence," Schultheis said, "as the northern elite is far from making unity attractive for the south."[17]

At the time when I first met him (July 2012), Fr. Schultheis had begun developing strategies aimed at helping build up both campuses in Juba and Wau. South Sudan achieved its independence from Sudan in July 2011, and he was hopeful that this would enable the University to develop at a faster pace. I was impressed by Fr. Schultheis' work. He was 83 years old at that time, but he was still going strong! He seemed to be a very spiritual man and had a wacky sense of humor! I felt encouraged by his zeal and love for the South Sudanese people; I felt God calling me to deeply give my life to those people. Fr. Schultheis died in 2017.

* * *

After Fr. Schultheis' departure, next came Fr. Mahdi Seif Aziz,

---

[17] Lefevere Patricia, "Catholic university launches in Sudan" *National Catholic Reporter*, November 11, 2010.

SJ a Jesuit from Egypt. He had lived in Wau for four years as a volunteer in the 1980s before he became a Jesuit. The experience he had in the 1980s confirmed his wish to become a Jesuit priest. He had brought some Near Eastern youth to visit Wau. This was an annual programme that had been going on for some years.

In the 1980s, when Fr. Seif came to Wau for the first time, the trip was organized by Fr. Henri Boulad, SJ who had a keen interest in making a difference in the poverty stricken southern Sudan. He is strongly committed to serving the poor, both Christians and Muslims, a commitment that continues with his work at Caritas. From 1984 to 1995 he was director of Caritas Egypt and President of Caritas North Africa and the Middle East. From 1991 to 1995 he was vice president of Caritas International for the Middle East and North Africa. Br. Herbert Liebl, SJ, whom I met in Rumbek, told me a lot of stories about Fr. Boulad and his love for the poor.

Many young people from Egypt came to Wau in the 1980s to work as youth ministers, teach in secondary schools, and help in other pastoral ministries for a few years. Some of these youth, like Fr. Seif, became priests and nuns. Fr. Seif was trying to imitate what Fr. Boulad did in the 1980s but in a small way. In this initiative, he worked closely with the Comboni Missionary Sisters. The youth came to camp in Wau, and did some activities in various parishes and other institutions for about a month. Some of them remained for a longer time, and some planned to come back in future to do some work as their contribution towards helping the poor.

The young people who came that year were from Egypt, Syria, and Lebanon. They travelled all the way from Juba to Wau by road taking about three days on that 700 kilometers journey. The roads were almost impassable because of the rainy season in which they came.

The young people were moved by the poverty they saw, and some of them vowed to come back to be part of making the lives of the people of Wau better. They were surprised by the kind of Arabic that was spoken in Wau. After three weeks in the town, they said that they could hardly find a person who spoke proper Arabic! The Arabic spoken in Wau was colloquial. It was known as Arabic Juba.

I was happy to meet these young people from affluent Egypt who still had the desire to make a deference in the lives of people in marginalized areas. I felt challenged to give myself even more to the people of South Sudan. I gave thanks to God for the privilege I had had of living a fairly normal life without much material depravation and violence that the children of South Sudan were experiencing.

* * *

During my stay in Wau, the Jesuits there had a good working relationship with the Catholic Health Training Institute (CHTI) which was ran by a consortium of nuns and priests from different religious congregations. They were known as the Solidarity with South Sudan (SSS). CHTI was found on the western Bank of the Jur River. The SSS mission statement read:

> "Inspired by the 2004 Rome Congress on Consecrated Life, Passion for Christ Passion for Humanity, this project, Solidarity with South Sudan (SSS or Solidarity), is an act of solidarity between religious institutes of men and women, which are members of the Unions of Superior Generals (USG

and UISG), and the Church in South Sudan under the direction of the Sudan Catholic Bishops' Conference (SCBC). After decades of civil war, when the Comprehensive Peace Agreement (CPA) was signed in January 2005, the bishops of South Sudan invited the USG/UISG to consider the needs of their people. Following a consultative process, it became clear that projects related to education, health, and pastoral care are needed if the goals of the CPA are to be achieved."[18]

The SSS people in Wau seemed to be very organized. Their compound was very impressive with attractive lawns. The Institute was built by the Germans in the 1970s and was destroyed during the second Sudanese civil war in the 1980s and 1990s. The SSS people came and restored the place in 2007. The quality of the buildings there was high with the classes, offices and other facilities well built. One could hardly believe that such buildings could be found in Wau. It was an impressive spectacle.

The Institute offered training for nurses. They had a diploma program that ran for three years. The SSS in Wau also helped to run the Daniel Comboni Hospital where their students learned practical skills. They were later involved in an impressive agricultural project on the banks of the Jur River which passes on the edge of the Institute. This project provided for the needs of the institution and also served as a demonstration center for the local people who were interested in learning modern methods of farming. Loyola would later borrow farming ideas from them.

---

[18] Solidarity with South Sudan Charter.

The SSS, as I saw it, was a new way of being Church in the sense that people from different affiliations could come together in order to work and share their religious vocations. This was very attractive to me. The SSS run a couple of other institutions in other parts of South Sudan such as Juba, Yambio, Rimenze, and Malakal. They were a sign of hope. They modeled solidarity; they reminded me of the need for collaborative ministry. When men and women, lay and ordained come together, there is a possibility of making a difference in people's lives rather than acting alone.

* * *

Later in 2012, another inspiring man arrived in Wau. Fr. Bernard Mallia, SJ, a Maltese Jesuit, who had worked in Sudan and South Sudan for over 25 years, joined the Jesuit community in Wau. Fr. Mallia had served for more than 20 years as a seminary professor at St. Paul Seminary in Juba and later on in Khartoum. He was also the librarian of the Seminary all that time. He was one of the living legends of the Sudan Jesuit mission.

In 1991, five years after Fr. Mallia's arrival in Juba, the Seminary had to be moved to Khartoum from Juba because of intense civil war in the south. Around that time, many Church personnel had been abducted by the SPLA. In 1987, Jesuit Fathers Salvador Ferrão and Joseph Pullicino were abducted by the SPLA in the Tore area of Yei. They spent three months in captivity. I will recount the story of the capture of these Jesuits later in this narrative. For the moment, it suffices to say that a year later, in 1988, three American Maryknoll Sisters were also kidnaped for a few days by the SPLA while working in a village near Juba. Monsignor Guissepe Pellerino, MCCJ, the Apostolic Administrator of the Diocese of Rumbek was also abducted by the SPLA around that time and spent one hundred days in captivity. Such abductions were on the increase, and the general security situation was not promising.

One day, on his way to the town of Yei to retrieve some theology books left behind by the two abducted Jesuits mentioned above, Fr. Mallia found himself in a crossfire between the rebels and the government soldiers, but he got away. He oversaw the move of the Seminary library from Juba to Khartoum in 1991. This was a very demanding task. He described what he experienced in Juba at that time in the following way:

> "It is only in 1990 that the war came close to us when the SPLA forces started shelling the town and harassing the people in the outskirts of Juba where our Seminary was located though they never came to us. Often at night, we would experience heavy shooting between Khartoum government forces and the SPLA forces so that the sky over us would be covered by a veritable rain of red tracer bullets. In the morning during classes, we would often hear land mines nearby being set off by some passing cow. The students became very disturbed, and so in 1991 we had to shift the Seminary to Khartoum."[19]

After retiring from the seminary in 2006, Fr. Mallia went for his sabbatical a year in Zambia at the Jesuit Center for

---

[19] Recollection by Fr. Bernard Mallia, SJ on June 22, 2013.

Theological Reflection (JCTR) in Lusaka and in Zimbabwe at Silveira House in Harare. These are two social justice centers for the Jesuits in Southern Africa. Fr. Mallia had gone there in order to learn how those centers worked with a view of beginning one such center in Juba. This was a worthwhile vision because of the political challenges that faces South Sudan at the moment.

After his sabbatical year Fr. Mallia went to Rumbek where he became pastor and chaplain at Rumbek Secondary School. He renovated the chapel there which was destroyed during the war. He began the Holy Cross Chaplaincy that served the students of Rumbek Secondary School and the young people around Rumbek town.

Rumbek Secondary School was first established in 1948 south of Malakal the then capital of the Upper Nile region. It was the first and the only secondary school in the whole of southern Sudan. It was later transferred to Rumbek by the Anglo-Egyptian colonial authorities. The school soon became one of the top three schools in the Sudan. It was for a long time considered as the "Cambridge of southern Sudan." It was very difficult to be admitted into the school, one had to be exceptional. Most of the South Sudanese elites such as Vice President James Wani Igga were educated there.

Fr. Mallia taught Christian Religious Education at Rumbek Secondary School for several years until he left Rumbek in 2012. The standard of education there at that time was very poor. This was because of lack of trained teachers and also because of the ravages of the two civil wars. The glory of the school had been, as it were, swept away by the wars. Fr. Mallia found it very difficult to teach there because the students were very rowdy.

On his arrival in Wau, Fr. Mallia was engaged in pastoral work at Holy Trinity Church at Jebel Kheir, where Fr. Vitus Sedlmair, SJ a German Jesuit had earlier worked. The Belanda people at that church incorporated elements of their traditional culture into their liturgy. The liturgy at that church was always animated by vigorous dancing and with loud and skillful drumming. On Easter Sunday 2014, I wrote the following in my journal about the liturgy at that church:

> "The dancing that took place on Easter Sunday at Jebel Kheir chapel was breathtaking! The drum being the center of focus, the Christians danced until things almost fell apart. Dancing and blowing traditional whistles are at the heart of the liturgy at that chapel. The man who did the drumming was particularly gifted, that was his art, and he did it well. The most interesting dancers were some three old men who staged quite peculiar moves that made them the heroes of the day. There were several traditional Belanda rituals that were performed throughout the Mass. The one that seemed to have captured the attention of most people was a ritual for reconciliation. At the time of the ritual, some old men came to the drum and did a few symbolic acts; then after a short while, women came running in from all corners throwing leaves in the air while sprinkling water. They blessed the crowd of people who came towards the drum dancing. Then, this was followed by an elaborate dance in circles. Later on, there was a special dance for welcoming Jesus back

from the dead, which was preceded by another small ritual."[20]

I liked the inculturated liturgies at that church. The people there showed me the value of keeping one's cultural practices and cultural identity alive even though they had embraced Christianity and its values and practices. Christianity is not necessarily against traditional cultures. Christianity and traditional culture can coexist fruitfully.

The interior of the Holy Trinity Church at Jebel Kheir was fascinating. Behind the sanctuary, there was a beautiful drawing depicting the baptism of Jesus by John the Baptist with the Holy Spirit descending from heaven. Both Jesus and John the Baptist were portrayed as local Belanda Bviri people. On the sides of the church, the walls were dominated by nicely done portraits of two great Sudanese saints: Daniele Comboni and Josephine Bakhita. A local artist painted those works of art. These were evidence of the great potential that could be found in a place where very little resources are available. I felt God calling me to be creative in my life. Every situation I find myself in is an opportunity to be creative.

Saint Josephine Bakhita deserves special attention because she is the first local Sudanese Christian to be made a saint in the Catholic Church. She was born in 1869 to a wealthy family in the Darfur region of the Sudan.[21] She belonged to the Daju ethnic group that is found around the town of Nyala. Arab slave traders kidnaped her at age nine. She was given the name *Bakhita*, which means *lucky*, by the slavers. She was sold and

---

[20] My Journal entry on April 24, 2014.

[21] Pope Benedict XVI, Saved in Hope: Encyclical Letter of the Supreme Pontiff Benedict XVI. (Vatican City: Ignatius Press, 2008), number 3.

resold in the markets in the towns of El Obeid and Khartoum. Bakhita was finally purchased in 1883 by Callisto Legnani, an Italian consul who planned to free her. She accompanied Legnani to Italy in 1885 and worked as a caregiver for the family of Augusto Michieli. She was treated well in Italy and grew to love the country. She became a Christian in 1890, and entered the Institute of Canossian Daughters of Charity in Venice, Italy in 1893. She served as a Canossian Sister for the next fifty years. Her gentle presence, her warm, amiable voice, and her willingness to help with any menial task were a comfort to the poor and suffering people who came to the door of the Institute. On October 1, 2000, she was canonized by Pope John Paul II. Saint Bakhita's life continued to be an inspiration to me as I shared my life with the South Sudanese people.

* * *

Food scarcity was a huge problem in Wau. This prompted the Jesuits to do something to help the students at Loyola Secondary School cope. In mid-October 2012, we began a feeding program for the students and staff. There was a need to provide some food for the students because most of them ate very little before coming to school. Hence, they could not concentrate on their studies because they were feeling hungry all the time. The students were happy that they could have some tea and bread at 10:00 a.m. We later initiated an agricultural project in the school's land that would produce food for students.

* * *

As I mentioned earlier, it was very difficult to get teachers in

Wau. Even the teachers who worked at the school were very unpredictable. Most of them were still students at the University of Bahr el Ghazal, and thus they were always on the move. The only reliable teachers at the school were the seven Jesuits who worked full-time. It was difficult to get regular teachers since very few teachers in South Sudan at that time were trained. Because of the unforeseen departure of teachers, some of the subjects were not taught for many weeks. It was an appalling situation. It was very common for a teacher to appear in the office and say that he or she was leaving town the following day. Lack of trained teachers was a huge problem in Wau and South Sudan in general. It was even more difficult to find female teachers even though Loyola's population was 50% girls. It was not easy to get female teachers in South Sudan because few women were educated.

The generosity of well-wishers is a blessing to the people of South Sudan. Without donations, it is difficult to run an institution in a situation like the one in South Sudan. In early December 2012, we learned that our request for a donation from the *Fundus Apostolicus et Caritativus Societatis Iesu* (FACSI) in Rome had been approved. FACSI is the solidarity fund for the Society of Jesus. We were awarded 26,000 Euros to purchase new text books for the school and to get internet connection. That internet access would help the teaching staff at Loyola to get supplementary resources for teaching, a novelty for a school in South Sudan. The books that were going to be acquired would be helpful in 2013 when we began to implement the new South Sudan curriculum.

The new curriculum was partly Kenyan and partly Ugandan. The Government of South Sudan (GOSS) had not succeeded to print the textbooks for the new curriculum. Thus, most of the books were purchased from Kenya and Uganda. We had heard rumors that new text books designed for the new South Sudan Curriculum had been ordered by the GOSS and were being printed in China. However, the books never arrived. I will say more about that curriculum later on in this story.

The author preparing to go to teach a class at
Loyola Secondary School in 2013.

Fr. Francis Njuguna, SJ (locally known as Deng Malual) at work with
some local women at the Multi-Educational Agricultural Jesuit Institute
of South Sudan (MAJIS) in the village of Akol Jal in Rumbek in 2012.

Loyola Secondary School community in 2008.

Fr. Michael Schultheis, SJ the founder of the Catholic University of South Sudan giving communion at a Mass in Juba.

Fr. Norman Dickson, SJ the founder of Loyola Secondary School at work in 1984

Celebrating the Feast of St. Ignatius of Loyola 2013 at Loyola Secondary School.

Students are heading to class after morning assembly at Loyola Secondary School.

Morning prayer at Loyola Secondary School in 2014

Chinese UN soldiers with some Loyola Secondary School students during a visit to the UN compound in Wau in 2012.

Wau Jesuit community members in August 2012 at the Jesuit residence.

Br. Herbert Liebl, SJ (centre) renovating the Jesuit church in Rumbek with the help of two local men after years of destruction during the second Sudanese civil war.

Chapter Six

Things Fall Apart

"One hopes that if one acts from a thirst for justice and suffers the consequences, then others may be spared the terror of disesteem and persecution."

John Howard Griffin

Ethnic tension has always been part of the lives of the people in and around Wau since the independence of the Sudan from the Anglo-Egyptian condominium rule in 1956. The Dinka and the so called "Fertit" group have always found something to cause tension among themselves. Wau has been an ethnic battlefield that has claimed many lives throughout the years.

Towards the end of 2012, the Christian Life Community (CLC) in Wau had organized a big youth meeting at the amphitheater of Wau's magnificent St. Mary's Cathedral. They had invited people from all walks of life to come and address the youth of Wau. That event was a way of reaching out to the many young Christians of Wau to help them cope with the challenges of life.

CLC is an international association of lay Christians. CLC draws its inspiration from the teachings of Saint Ignatius of

Loyola and receives spiritual guidance from the Jesuits. The experience of going through a profound prayer program outlined in the *Spiritual Exercises* of Saint Ignatius is of paramount importance to the members of the CLC. Members of CLC are encouraged to adhere to a lifestyle which is simple and based on the Gospel message. Service to the poor and the integration of contemplation and action are hallmarks of the CLC way of life.

The group was started in Wau in 2008 by the Jesuits. Many lay people around Wau had been fascinated by this way of life, and the impact that the group was having in the communities in Wau was impressive. The CLC people were active in promoting a faith that does justice in Wau. They walked the talk. I was impressed by them and was inspired to live out my faith in radical ways as the CLC people were doing.

* * *

On the evening of the first day of the youth event, at around 7:00 p.m., the Jesuit animator of CLC in Wau, was returning from the meeting at the Cathedral on the Loyola Secondary School Land Cruiser. He met a group of rowdy youths blocking the way off Wau-Bussere road.

At first, the Jesuit thought that that was the normal crowd which gathered there every evening to watch other young people play football. He drove slowly as he approached the crowd. Suddenly, he realized that all the attention of those young people was on him, and they seemed to be out of control. When they got out machetes and other weapons, the Jesuit knew that things had fallen apart. They immediately started to attack him. One huge wooden post was used to hit the front of the car. They kept on shouting at the Jesuit and eventually the situation turned into anarchy. He managed to somehow drive past the crowd. The crowd followed him while throwing huge stones and machetes towards the car. One machete got into the car, and it almost hit the Jesuit.

He eventually managed to navigate the small alleyways of the Jebel Kheir suburb and found his way up to Loyola Secondary School. He was scared to the bones. He got into the house running and shouting for help. One Loyola Secondary School teacher who had come to visit the Jesuits was advised to stay for the night at the Jesuit house because the rowdy and blood-thirsty young people had blocked all the roads.

That night we heard a lot of gunfire coming from as close as the Loyola Secondary School football field. It was very scary because at that time the school was not fenced and anyone could access the school compound from any direction. Luckily, we had a policeman who guarded the property at night. Some of us retired to bed early closing all the windows which were most of the time left open because of the heat. The following morning gunshots continued to be heard, and we decided not to venture out of our Jesuit compound.

A few days later the road leading out from Jebel Kheir to Wau town was completely barricaded by soldiers and all vehicles attempting to pass there were returned. We were virtually cut off from Wau town for about a week.

Ten people were killed on December 7, 2012, after a group of protesting youth was fired at with live bullets by the SPLA soldiers. The *Sudan Tribune* reported the following:

> "In the late hours of Saturday, the South Sudan's army (SPLA) moved in to remove road blocks that

had been created in protest against the relocation of a local council to a nearby area (Bagari), the United Nations Mission in South Sudan said. Speaking to Al Jazeera, the mission's Director of Communications and Public Information, Liam McDowall, said UNMISS had received reports that six people were killed when the army opened fire on those protesting against the army dismantling the road blocks on Saturday. On Sunday morning, protesters moved into Wau town, apparently in an attempt to deliver a petition listing their grievances to the Governor. Troops again fired on the crowd killing four more people, McDowall said."[22]

* * *

The violence narrated above, begun simmering for months before a sudden explosion of anger erupted on that December day. There was some information that went around about a plan to move the headquarters of Wau County out of Wau town and establish it in a small and impoverished village of Bagari which was about 10 kilometers northwest of Wau. Bagari village had no social amenities and was somewhat backward. This move was imminent in December 2012.

The local Belanda people, who were the majority in Wau town, felt that the Dinka people from the Warap region were using the move of the county headquarters as a pretext of taking over the town from them. The Dinka seemed to have dominated most of the government positions in the town. The Belanda felt that they were being pushed out of a town which they

---

[22] See *Sudan Tribune* Sunday December 9, 2012.

considered as their home. Bagari, according to the Dinka, was where the Belanda belonged.

Other non-Dinka ethnic groups joined the Belanda in the fight against the Dinka to prevent the move of Wau County into the village. The violence quickly turned out to be a Fertit - Dinka revenge and counter-revenge. As I mentioned earlier in this narrative, historically, the non-Dinka ethnic groups in Wau which were collectively known as the "Fertit" by the Arabs, were always antagonistic toward the Dinka. History seemed to be repeating itself that December.

The violence continued for three days unabated. Some Ugandan trucks ferrying merchandise for sale in Wau town, from the town of Yambio and beyond, were attacked some five kilometers out of Wau on the Wau-Bussere road. The trucks were burnt down by an angry group of youth, and all the merchandise was looted or burnt.

Some United Nations Mission in South Sudan (UNMISS) trucks were seen moving up and down in the town, but they did not take any side during the violence. They only collected information of what was happening. Many indiscriminate arrests by the police of Belanda men took place.

It was feared that the ring leader of the Belanda youth, who started the agitation, was taken one night to the forests close to the garrison town of Mapel and was executed. Many Belanda men disappeared. Soldiers were brought in from the neighboring towns of Rumbek and Kuajok. They came into Wau singing war songs. Some of these soldiers were deployed to Bagari village. They passed on the Bagari road close to Loyola chanting war songs. It was a scary scene. Many people died in the first few days of the violence, most of them were Belanda. Some of them were buried in a cemetery which is about a kilometer from Loyola. We thought that the violence would erupt during that burial, but nothing happened on that day.

A 6:00 p.m. to 6:00 a.m. curfew was imposed. From that time on, curfews became a common occurrence it the town of Wau. Months after the violence one could meet many soldiers on the road beginning at 9:00 p.m. Many people were arrested in Wau at that time for breaking the curfew. Those arrested would spend the night at a military barracks and received strokes of the cane the following morning and set free. Most of the soldiers who patrolled the town at night looked so drunk.

In March 2013, some of the soldiers implementing the curfew on Wau town made Loyola Secondary School their operating base. They would apprehend anyone who tried to cross over the hill to the other side after 9:00 p.m. They were a nuisance to the Jesuits because they demanded to be given clean water, food, and also a room to sleep. Those soldiers who were resident in the school brought back to the people of Jebel Kheir memories of the second Sudanese civil war when the school was a garrison.

* * *

On December 21, 2012, Bishop Rudolf Deng Majak wrote a pastoral letter condemning the violence. It partly read:

> "My brothers and sisters, during the last two weeks our town of Wau has witnessed the tragic, deadly events of untold sufferings, destruction and death that has shocked us all into shame and utter disbelief! Our brothers and sisters in the villages of

Bagari, Farajalla and Hai Fellata in particular live in utter desolation and dispossession. The spirit of tribalism or ethnic based strife, revenge and counter revenge is taking the upper hand. It was only seventeen months ago that we gained our independence on July 9, 2011, a very great price of more than two million dead! Many of us thought that our real enemy was in Khartoum. With disbelief and consternation, we ourselves are real enemy with our tribal conflicts, superiority complex, arrogance, robbery, greed, corruption, exclusiveness and pride. The killing and destruction of the last two weeks cannot be justified at all. The infighting whether ethnically or politically motivated must stop. […] my appeal to all the faithful and citizens of our Diocese is to stop violence and communal strife. Promote instead the value of peace and communion as Christmas is approaching. Let us stand up to the principles of Christian harmony and forgiveness to welcome Christ the Prince of Peace and let the songs of the angels come true in our hearts."[23]

It was claimed at that time that the move of the counties from towns to the villages was the wish of Dr. John Garang after the Comprehensive Peace Agreement (CPA) in 2005. The idea was that this would help the government focus on the development of the villages. This was a good idea if it was not politicized and ethnicized as it was in the case of what happened in Wau in 2012. It seemed to me that the idea had been manipulated

---

[23] Pastoral letter of Bishop Rudolf Deng Majak of the Diocese of Wau on December 21, 2012 on the inter-ethnic violence in Wau.

and that was the cause of all the violence and bloodshed that was witnessed at that time in Wau.

The police and the military were also divided along ethnic lines. It was said that some sections of the police and military were disarmed, but they quickly brought out the illegal arms that they had in their houses. Many influential Belanda people were detained in the CID offices in Wau for many weeks.

The United Nation Mission in South Sudan (UNMISS) compound near Wau airport was flooded with people fleeing from the fighting. On December 20, 2012, the following was reported on the UN website:

> "The United Nations peacekeeping operation in South Sudan reports that the situation in the town of Wau remains tense following the arrival of some 5,000 people seeking safety at a UN base there yesterday amidst violence and protests that began last week after government officials said they would move the seat of local government out of Wau to the nearby village of Bagari. "Earlier today, many of those who sought UN protection and had stayed overnight left the base to inspect their homes, a significant number of civilians, mainly women, children and the elderly, remain in the UN base and continue to be protected," added the spokesperson, Eduardo Del Buey, in a news briefing at UN Headquarters in New York. Mr. Del Buey added that UN humanitarian agencies stand ready to provide assistance, and that UNMISS is urging authorities and community leaders to "exercise restraint and

engage in peaceful dialogue in order to prevent a further deterioration of the fragile situation.""[24]

* * *

About a week and a half after the intense three days fight in early December 2012, news came to us that some people had been found dead in a forest south of Loyola in a place called Farajalla. Their bodies had been brought to Wau Teaching Hospital on December 15. Because we were planning to leave Wau, in the morning of December 16, 2012, for Rumbek, we were advised to do so as early as we could.

We had a safe but rough journey to Rumbek on December 16, 2012. We passed many checkpoints without being asked to produce our passports because Maltese Jesuit, Fr. Bernard Mallia, spoke in the Dinka language with the military people at the checkpoints. The Dinka soldiers were fascinated to see a white man speaking their language. Thus, they let us go through the checkpoints without much ado.

We had one scaring experience during that journey. As we arrived in Rumbek, an SPLA truck full of armed soldiers pulled up close to our Land Cruiser. The soldiers were carrying rounds and rounds of ammunition, and this scared a hell out of us. One Jesuit had covered his head with an Islamic headscarf to prevent him from being overwhelmed by the dust coming into the car as he drove. An SPLA soldier quickly saw him and ordered him to get out of the car. The SPLA man furiously told the Jesuit to get off the headscarf. The military man warned him not to do it again.

---

[24] See UN News Center, "The Situation in Wau, South Sudan."
http://www.un.org/apps/news/story.asp?NewsID=43824#.U_1ZAvldWH4.

The Arabs were hated in Rumbek, and any trace of Arabic culture was loathed with a special passion. There was a long battle that was fought between the SPLA and the Arab military from Khartoum, during the second Sudanese civil war, before the SPLA took Rumbek. The Arabs did not like the Dinka of Rumbek because they were fierce and rebellious to Arab rule. There was a school in Rumbek that had its name as Agelgum. It was named after a Dinka woman warrior who gave a lot of trouble to the Arab soldiers by her acts of valor during the war.

On our arrival at the Jesuit house in Rumbek, we got information that Wau was on fire. Fighting had broken out again. A school on the Rumbek-Wau road near Mbili had been attacked, and the people who were sheltering there were murdered.

President Salva Kiir Mayardit came to Wau on December 21, 2012. He asked the people to accept the relocation of Wau County headquaters to Bagari village. He said that that action would bring services close to the people. The President's speech seemed heavy handed to the local people. He said that he could have "done the same thing" if he was in a similar situation. This angered the non-Dinka ethnic groups.

* * *

After the violence ended, Wau town was for months manned by soldiers from neighboring counties. They were ready to lash anyone numerous strokes of the cane on slight provocation. Reckless motorbike riders and idlers were their easy target. Anyone who was found recklessly riding a motorbike or idling around would be ordered to lie down on the side of a dusty road, and he would be lashed many strokes of a cane.

The violence of December 2012 caused some Dinka students at Loyola to transfer to other schools because Loyola was situated in an area dominated by the Belanda people. Most of the students at Loyola were Belanda. It became insecure for the Dinka students to walk up to Loyola through the cluster of houses below the little hill on which Loyola Secondary School is located.

I had never been in a situation where automatic gunfire had gone on throughout the day and night. I experienced that for the first time in Wau. I contemplated sleeping on the floor to avoid being hit by a stray bullet while I was sleeping on my bed. However, even amidst all that violence, I continued to feel God's loving presence. God continued to reassure me that my work in South Sudan was valuable and I was helping build the reign of God there by my presence and care to the people I was called to serve. I was a witness the Gospel values of compassion, love, hope and standing with the oppressed people who needed to be reassured of God's abiding presence and love for them amidst difficult circumstances.

Chapter Seven

There and Back

"Well, you say, 'where am I to be? Nowhere, according to you! And you will be quite right! 'Nowhere' is where I want you! Why, when you are 'nowhere' physically, you are "everywhere spiritually."

The Cloud of the Unknowing

Wau and Rumbek are two different worlds in many ways. Although Wau is more urban than Rumbek, the two towns are similar in lack of infrastructure and basic amenities such as water and electricity. If Charles Dickens lived in the Bahr el Ghazal in the twenty first century, he could have written a tale of two cities depicting the inner struggles of the folks who live in Rumbek and Wau.

I was happy to be back in Rumbek in mid-December 2012. The insecurity in Wau had made life there to be very scary; it was good to be in a relatively peaceful place. It was also good to change the environment for rest and recuperation after months of hard work in a rather difficult environment.

One blessing that I kept experiencing as I continued living and travelling inside South Sudan is that I continued to meet heroic men and women whose zeal for that country kept my hopes alive. In Rumbek at that time, I met Fr. Salvador Ferrão, SJ a Goan Jesuit who I had not seen in my previous visit to Rumbek in July 2012. He was jovial and happy to see us; he welcomed us warmly. Fr. Ferrão was considered a prophet because he organized many peace and justice workshops in the diocese under the title *Cultivate Justice, Harvest Peace*. He was seen as a possible successor of the Late Bishop Ceazar Mazzolari, MCCJ of the Catholic Diocese of Rumbek, who was mentioned earlier. Fr. Ferrão worked as a parish priest for many years in Tabora, Tanzania. He also worked with the Jesuit Refugee Service (JRS) in Angola and other parts of Africa. At the time I met him, he grew a long beard, and he looked like an Indian *sanyasi*! Bishop Rudolf Deng Majak of Wau baptized Fr. Ferrão, *mulana*, which means "master" in Arabic.

In 1987, Fr. Ferrão together with Fr. Joseph Pullicino, SJ, a Maltese, spent three months in captivity. They were held by the Sudan People's Liberation Army (SPLA). At that time, 1986-1987, the Jesuit Fathers were ministering to the refugees in fourteen refugee camps in Tore, which is in the area of Yei, and they were also running the parish there. These refugees were mainly Ugandans who had fled the war that was going on in that country at that time. Fr. Pio Ciampa, SJ, an Italian, was part of the mission team there, but the SPLA men did not capture him on that fateful day.

During the three months of their captivity, the Jesuits roamed the bushes of southern Sudan. They had a variety of difficult experiences. Fr. Pullicino almost died of malaria. The SPLA men allowed the priests to baptize children and celebrate Mass. One incident during that eventful journey needs to be recounted here. On September 6, 1987, the fathers reached an abandoned parish in Chukudum in the Diocese of Torit (DOT). Fr. Ferrão recalled the day:

> "At Chukudum, where there was a parish which was destroyed three years earlier, we met another priest who was living among villagers and cutoff completely from the world by the war. He was poorly dressed, having no sandals and not knowing what was going to happen. He lived in the hills with the people. We asked him to join us on our long walk to the unknown. In a partly destroyed church, we celebrated Mass for a few Christians who had come from the hills to pray. The priests were so shabbily dressed; the altar was shabby too. The Christians were better dressed than the priests. It was a simple but admirable sight."[25]

A few days before the above incident, the Fathers met women and children in an abanboned village. Fr. Ferrão remembered the incident in the following manner:

> "In another village, we saw many children and I asked one of their mothers whether they were baptized or not. She told me they were not but they would like their children to be baptized. I asked permission from the SPLA officer in charge, and we baptized 20 children, and gave them a note as a proof of baptism. We told them that their priest will not come until the end of the war. But God never forgets

---

[25] Recollection by Fr. Salvador Ferrão, SJ, March 2014.

God's people and has sent priests to baptize their children. The celebration of baptism ended with a song to Our Lady."[26]

The mission of the Jesuits at Tore came to an end with the abduction of the two priests in July 1987. Fr. Ciampa managed to escape to Aba in Zaire (now Democratic Republic of Congo) where he got safe passage to Nairobi, Kenya in a small chartered plane. The abducted Fathers were set free at the Kenyan border at Lokichoggio three months later, where the International Red Cross received them. Twenty years later, in 2006, Fr. Ferrão met the Commanding Officer, who ordered the abduction in Rumbek. The SPLA man apologized for what he did to the priests, and they were reconciled.

At the time I met him in Rumbek, Fr. Ferrão was the Parish Priest of St. Teresa Mission of Reconciliation Church in Rumbek. He had also begun a small mission in the Alor *payam* (district) which is about 110 kilometers northeast of Rumbek town. Alor *payam* is found in the Maper County. The area is prone to inter-ethnic clashes and cattle raiding escapades among the Nuer, Pakam, and Luac-Jang communities. Fr. Ferrão helped to build a chapel, a dispensary and a primary school in the area. He hoped that these institutions, however small, would help transform the area and contribute to peace. He was beginning what is called "primary evangelization" because there were hardly any Catholics in the area. He collaborated closely with the Episcopal Church of South Sudan (ECS) priests who were working in the area. Fr. Ferrão would visit Maper for weeks on end, most of the time sleeping in a tent. This was before he was able to build a little house there.

---

[26] Recollection by Fr. Salvador Ferrão, SJ, March 2014.

During the rainy season, Alor was inaccessible and, thus, it was cut off from Rumbek. Fr. Ferrão could not manage to go there during the rains.

Fr. Ferrão is a real man for the frontiers, and I was encouraged by his zeal to spread the Gospel message in the frontiers where others do not want to go. He was a living embodiment of someone who lived the joy of the Gospel. He never vacillated in his quest to be an authentic disciple. I got a lot of inspiration from him to be a foot soldier for Christ.

* * *

One afternoon during that visit to Rumbek, Fr. Francis Njuguna took me for the first time to visit the Multi-Educational Agricultural Jesuit Institute of South Sudan (MAJIS). The project began on a piece of land that was donated by some Dinka chiefs in the village of Akol Jal some 11 kilometers from Rumbek town. These chiefs had approached the Diocese of Rumbek (DOR) with a desire of having a school in their area. In turn, DOR approached the Jesuits to inquire if they were in a position to take up the challenge. After a long period of discernment, and considering the desires of the Dinka Chiefs who donated the land, the Jesuits decided to start an agricultural school there.

Fr. Njuguna was the first Jesuit to be sent there as the director of the project. He was a pathfinder for that mission. He had studied Environmental Science in India, and had a great interest in agriculture and the environment. On his arrival at the farm Fr. Njuguna quickly began fencing the whole area, which is about two square kilometers, to prevent the local people from encroaching on the land. He then established a relationship with the local Dinka people who lived near the farm. Fr. Njuguna had immersed himself fully into the local situation, he shared his life with the local people in a culture that was different from his. His was a theology that began with praxis. He discerned the desires of the people of God and started his work from there. He was popular among the local people, who gave him a Dinka name, Deng Malual. Malual means a white (read brown) person in the Dinka language. Fr. Njuguna was given this name because of his light complexion. Apart from working on the farm, he was always called upon by the Dinka chiefs to mediate in village matters such as marriage and communal feuds.

At that time, December 2013, Fr. Njuguna was trying to set up farm buildings and classrooms for the future agricultural school. Getting a good contactor for the project was difficult. He was frustrated by some officials in Rumbek town who wanted Fr. Njuguna to award a local man the building contract. It was clear that the local man could not manage to carry out the project. He had a very bad track record. Eventually, because of the pressure from the officials at Rumbek, the man was given a down payment to start building. Within a week, the man had disappeared with the money and could not be seen in Rumbek for many months.

At the time of my visit, some workers were making building blocks for the future institute. There was a borehole that had been dug, and it provided enough water for the building project and for the local people to use. It was a very difficult and expensive task to begin the construction work. It was difficult to get building materials and also to get the right people to do the construction work. The local chief had also asked Fr. Njuguna to employ some local youth on the building site. That was also difficult because some local youth were lazy and would disappear from time to time. On the day of my visit, I met some young people standing near the construction site. They quickly noticed that I was a newcomer, and they got interested in me. They came close to where I was standing and began to speak to me in the Dinka language. I did not respond to them because I could not understand what they were saying, and that angered some of them who started shouting at me.

As the construction was beginning, Fr. Njuguna continued to set up demonstration plots in which he would teach local women how to plant vegetables and other crops. Some of the women were very enthusiastic about the new experience. The Dinka people are nomadic cattle keepers, and growing crops was a new experience for them. Perhaps if they can learn how to farm, they will not put much emphasis on getting as many herds of cattle as they can from cattle raiding escapades. Thus, that project can help reduce the inter-clan fighting that is common in Rumbek sometimes because of cattle raiding. In that way, the farm school can be a source of peace and reconciliation by helping break down a vicious cycle of enmity. Fr. Njuguna had also started informal training seminars on modern crop planting methods. These seminars were done under a well-constructed grass thatched shade. The turnout was not very impressive but Fr. Njuguna did not give up; he continued giving these seminars to the locals.

The village of Akol Jal, where the farm is located, is in the midst of two rival Dinka clans. The two clans fight periodically. One day in January 2013, the construction workers had to be evacuated from the farm because of intense fighting. The fighting went on for about three weeks before the workers came back on site. They had to camp in the compound of the Jesuit community in Rumbek town for their safety. One dead body was later found on the farm; the police were called in to retrieve it. Later, a Polish Jesuit who worked in the farm school wrote the following:

> "Our neighborhood in Akol Jal has been affected by clan fighting in the recent weeks and months. Lately, there has been a lot of shooting in Akol Jal and in Pul Chum, which is four kilometers from Akol Jal on the road leading to the farm. The number people who have been shot dead in the area of Rumbek area and Akol Jal in the previous week is about fifteen. It is so sad. Following the advice of the people from Akol Jal, we do not stay too late in the afternoon and in the evening on the farm because of the perilous situation. We usually get out as early as we can."[27]

The hope of the Jesuits was that the Farm School would help unite the people around the farm who come from belligerent clans. The school would help them develop new ways of life that go beyond looking at each other as enemies.

There was also a lot of deforestation that was taking place around Rumbek. It was Fr. Njuguna's wish to do some environmental conservation training in the farm school. The hope was that some spiritual formation and other pastoral initiatives would begin once the farm was properly established.

The inculturation that Fr. Njuguna demonstrated was inspiring. He had made himself one with the people. He considered himself not a superior but as a facilitator. The

---

[27] Eastern Africa Jesuit News Update 14:29 July 18, 2014.

people of Akol Jal responded to that very well; he was welcomed as a member of the community who shared the joys and pain of the people. The people of Akol Jal invited him to be part of their village council that deliberated on the issues affecting the village. He challenged me to continue to immerse myself in the new culture and try to bring joy and hope to the people who for many years have endured suffering and the ravages of War.

Chapter Eight

Going Further Still

"Those who desire to show greater devotion and to distinguish themselves in total service to their eternal King and universal Lord, will not only offer their persons for the labor, but go further still. They will work against their human sensitivities and against their carnal and worldly love, and they will make offering of greater worth and moment."

St. Ignatius of Loyola (*Spiritual Exercises 97*)

Travelling in the South Sudanese roads is quite an adventure. One had to prepare himself or herself psychologically before attempting the epic journey inside terra incognita! Before I got on my way back to Wau from Rumbek in January of 2013, I feared that the roads were insecure. However, I was given a green light by some people who had recently travelled on that road. Moreover, some Mother Teresa Sisters had gone past Wau to Turalei, close to the contested oil-rich Abyei region, during that time. Therefore, I gained the confidence to go back after all the violence that had occurred in Wau. There were some killings on the Rumbek-Wau road, in and around the village town of Cueibet, but I was informed that these were connected to cattle raiding among the Dinka clans. The day after I left Rumbek, inter-clan violence broke out there, and it lasted for a few weeks.

My journey back to Wau at that time was torturous. The road was very rough, and we were crowded in the back of a Land Cruiser. A lot of luggage was piled in the sitting area. The driver of the Land Cruiser was cruising at a very high speed. It was like a rally competition. One woman had a bag of groundnuts on top of the Land Cruiser. The bag broke on our way, and we had to stop near the town of Cueibet to repack the groundnuts. Some of the passengers there started eating the groundnuts. A man who stood near me looked at me with much curiosity. Surprisingly, he took some nuts from the ground and gave them to me and told me to eat. That was a sign that he wanted to be at peace with me; a sign of his generosity to me.

During that journey, we had to stop at the SPLA checkpoints, which were about ten, on the Rumbek-Wau road. At one checkpoint an SPLA man asked for my passport, he was about 20 years old. He found that my visa was okay, and he then asked for money. I gave him the money and demanded a receipt. He was angry that I had requested a receipt, and he uttered some threatening remarks to me. There was a gun close to where he sat and, upon seeing it, I decided not to continue with the argument. Such checkpoints were common on most roads of South Sudan. I always wondered if some of those checkpoints were legitimate. Some of these checkpoints were about 10 kilometers of each other.

When I arrived back in Wau, I was happy because as I got out of the Land Cruiser at Souk Wau, it was clear to me that the town was at peace. The violence that began a month earlier had subsided. I was so grateful to God that I arrived back safely.

* * *

The registration of our students for their national examinations was delayed for a long time. They were supposed to have been registered in August 2012, but by the end of February 2013, nothing had happened. The education authorities in Khartoum did not honor the agreement between the Government of South Sudan (GOSS) in Juba and the Government of Sudan (GOS) in Khartoum to provide the Sudan School Certificate Examinations for four years after the independence of South Sudan. The education officials in Juba said that the government of Sudan in Khartoum had charged them exorbitant fees. That was a deliberate move to make it difficult for South Sudan to afford the cost of buying the examinations. It was an act of sabotage. Many negotiations took place, but no agreement between the two governments was reached by the beginning of 2013.

One day, a local journalist from Radio Miraya, a UN radio station, came to Loyola Secondary School and interviewed the Principal about the situation of the national examinations. The Principal spoke to the journalist openly saying how the students and teachers were frustrated and were uncertain about what was happening. The next day, Radio Miraya, aired what the Principal had said and added some commentary which was exaggerated.

On the day of the broadcast, some officials from the Ministry of Education in Wau arrived at Loyola. They looked visibly furious, and they asked to see the Principal. They questioned him on what he had said to the journalist for about an hour and a half. They seemed satisfied with what he said, and they then left the school.

At last, in late February 2013, we heard that the Ministry of Education in Juba had decided to set the examinations and were no longer depending on Khartoum to provide the examinations. What a relief it was! The students were happy to hear that good news. Living in uncertainty, not knowing what to expect the next day had become part of my life at that time.

At that time, the Minister of Education for the region, who was based in Wau, claimed that government in Khartoum had deceived South Sudan about the national examinations. He also complained that the Ministry of Education in Juba was pressuring the implementation of the new South Sudan syllabus in the whole country, yet there were no textbooks and teachers had not been trained how to teach the new syllabus. He seemed helpless and confused.

Our students finally did their examinations in April 2013, and they got an excellent result. Loyola Secondary School was the top school in Wau County and the third in Western Bahr el Ghazal region. Twenty-eight students from Loyola qualified to join universities in South Sudan. That was a great achievement for me. I felt for the first time that I had done something concrete for the future of South Sudan by contributing to the education of those young men and women who would shape the future of the new country.

There were rumors that the examinations had been sold in some markets in South Sudan and that they would be nullified. It was said that a car which was transporting the examinations to the town of Torit in the Eastern Equatoria State "got an accident" and the examinations were stolen and circulated in many parts of South Sudan. Others said that because the exams were set in Juba, they were not going to be recognized by Universities in South Sudan and around the world because the curriculum was designed in Khartoum and, thus, the examinations had to come from there and not from Juba. The marking of the examinations was also delayed in Juba because of lack of funds. All these uncertainties brought a lot of tension and fear in the students who had done the examinations. We later realized that most of the rumors were not true.

* * *

Developing infrastructure in South Sudan was always a difficult undertaking. Getting a good contactor was hard because they were very few. Additionally, building materials were far too expensive in the local markets and thus people had to import materials from other countries, yet the roads were in bad conditions. The roads were only passable during the dry season, when the rains arrived, people avoided long journeys because it was easy to get stuck for days in the mud-ridden roads.

The story below illustrates how difficult it was to develop infrastructure at Loyola Secondary School partly because of the difficult situation in the country. In mid-March 2013, a building contractor came to Wau to meet the Jesuits resident there. The contractor appeared to be very young perhaps in his early thirties. The purpose of that meeting was to sign a contract for the construction of four science laboratories: Physics, Chemistry, Biology and Computer Science.

Laboratories were a great need in the school because at that time all science subjects were taught theoretically. I found it tough to teach Biology and Chemistry because I could not demonstrate to the students some key practical activities. The news about the laboratories was sweet music to my ears!

The contractor had already made some architectural drawings of the proposed buildings. They looked impressive. We looked at the actual places that the buildings were to stand, and we made suggestions and amendments to the original plan. We were very hopeful that at last development of infrastructure in the school would begin. The contract was signed, and the contractor promised to begin the work in April 2013. The work was to be completed by October 2013. We spent a whole day discussing, evaluating and planning for the forthcoming buildings.

In April 2013, the contactor came with some builders together with his local foreman. They brought to the construction site some gravel and sand. They also cordoned off their working area and began building a retention wall that would help divert a road which was inside the building area. They also started digging up the foundation for the computer laboratory. After three weeks, it became clear that the contractor was not serious about the project. He spent most of his time away. He claimed that building materials were so expensive in Wau and that he was trying to buy the materials from out of the country and bring them by road to Wau.

Months came and went without any progress. The project turned out to be a huge disappointment to the Jesuits in Wau. One and a half years after the contract was signed the contractor only managed to make the Loyola Secondary School compound look untidy because of the unfinished buildings most of which were on their foundation level.

To build in South Sudan was very difficult because of the lack of building materials including other logistical challenges. Nonetheless, it was wise to choose the right people to do the work. One had to find out about the credibility of a contractor before signing a contract. Many other contractors in Wau disappeared without finishing the work they had started. Others just did poor work.

One thing that I learned while in Wau, from such experiences as the one narrated above, was to live in the hands of God in the face of unpredictable situations. I had just to trust in God and live a day at a time. I had to let go of my desire to plan and see those plans take effect.

Chapter Nine

Making Old Things New

"And no one pours new wine into old wineskins. If he does, the new wine will burst the skins, the wine will run out and the wineskins will be ruined."

Luke 5:37

Beginning a new project in the unpredictable situation of South Sudan proved to the most difficult thing one could imagine. One had to struggle to get anything new off the ground; everything seemed unpredictable. The lack of predictability strengthened people's faith in divine providence. Divine providence rightly describes what happened to us at Loyola Secondary School. Towards the end of February 2013, the school acquired about 3000 text books courtesy of funds received from generous donors of the school. Two Jesuits travelled to neighboring Kenya by road to buy the books because they were not available in South Sudan. They endured the rough terrain and it took them many days to be back. The arrival of the textbooks meant that we had to start implementing the new South Sudan curriculum immediately. That was good news for us.

We opened a new academic year at Loyola Secondary School on April 2, 2013. This was a new beginning at the school, a happy moment. We introduced the new South Sudan secondary school curriculum. After many years of trying, we had eventually succeeded! God was on our side. We initially introduced eleven subjects: Mathematics, English, Arabic, Chemistry, Physics, Biology, Geography, History, Agriculture, Commerce and Christian Religious Education. It was a four years' course rather than the three years that was required by the Sudan School Certificate syllabus made in Khartoum. The books that we had acquired from Nairobi were sufficient for us to implement the new syllabus.

The new syllabus was a lighter burden to the students compared to the old Khartoum syllabus that was described earlier. The senior one and senior two classes were required to take ten subjects rather than the previous sixteen subjects. The senior three and senior four classes were required to take only seven subjects in either the Sciences or the Arts. Moreover, the contents of the syllabus were considerate although it would require one more year to complete secondary school education.

The new South Sudan secondary school curriculum, was promulgated in 2005 after the signing of the Comprehensive Peace Agreement (CPA). However, it was not implemented because of lack of textbooks and trained teachers. Some schools had implemented the new syllabus as early as 2007 while others continued to follow the old syllabus from Khartoum. Other schools in the South Sudanese regions neighboring Kenya, Uganda, and Ethiopia, followed the syllabi of these countries and took national examinations from these countries. It was a chaotic situation. January 2014 marked the end of that confusion. The government required that all the schools in the country to use the new South Sudan syllabus as a guideline for instruction. This was ironical because there were still no textbooks designed for teaching that syllabus. Most schools used books bought from Kenya and Uganda.

Moreover, the curriculum had some lacunae. For example, there was no syllabus for Literature in English, yet the students who wanted to specialize in the Arts subjects were required to take Literature in English as a compulsory subject. In addition to this, the new syllabus also encouraged schools to teach a local language as part of preserving the South Sudanese cultural heritage. This proved impossible because there were no books for such languages and the teachers were not trained for such a scenario. Moreover, in a cosmopolitan place like Wau, where people spoke diverse local languages, it was difficult to select the local language to be taught at the school. The idea that a local language could be taught at Loyola raised a lot of emotions in the students because they thought that a specific local language was going to be imposed on them. The issue of a local language in the school was suspended because it proved to be too delicate to handle in such a multicultural setting.

The Jesuits in Rumbek were very generous to us at Loyola at the time when we were trying to implement the new school curriculum. They helped us find books which we did not have from Loreto Girls Secondary School in Rumbek. The Irish Loreto Sisters at Loreto Girls Secondary School in Rumbek had implemented the new curriculum in their school in 2008. They were an invaluable resource to us at Loyola.

As part of implementing the new curriculum at Loyola, we were able to do a teacher training exercise on the new syllabus. We explained to the teachers what was required, and we hoped that they would adapt as time went by. It was a very demanding task. We were lucky that we had acquired a soft copy of the whole new syllabus a year before we implemented it. This was very providential because it enabled us to carry out the training exercise with ease because we could easily print out the syllabi for each subject taught by each teacher rather than depend on the few syllabi book that were circulated by the Ministry of Education.

Apart from the syllabus, we handed to each of the teachers a copy of the textbooks and a teacher's guide for the subjects they were to teach. The teacher's guides helped the teachers to understand the dynamics of the new syllabus. We later learned, through follow up, that some teachers were still teaching the old syllabus. We had to tell them to stop that and stick to the new syllabus; things had changed. We understood that it was difficult for them because they were schooled in that syllabus.

We were also able to assist other schools around Wau that were interested in implementing the new syllabus. We gave advice and donated a few copies of the textbooks to other schools such as John Paul II Secondary School. Loyola was among the first schools in Wau to implement the new South Sudan curriculum, and thus Loyola became a resource center for other schools in Wau that were trying to implement the new curriculum. The Ministry of Education in Wau also asked us to help in training the teachers around Wau about the new syllabus.

This new syllabus was going to be rather intensive because it would require the students to master the content of all the four years in order to pass their national examinations at the end of the fourth year. It was going to be different from the Sudan School Certificate curriculum examination that focused only on the final third year work. It was common in the old curriculum to find students skipping a class in order to reach the third year then they would memorize that year's content in order to pass their examinations.

* * *

I was a teacher in a Jesuit school, but I did not know much about the Jesuit style education. Being a teacher in South Sudan needed me to be creative as well as have special skills that would help me be an effective teacher in that context. Consequently, in April of 2013, I travel to Nairobi to attend a Jesuit pedagogy meeting. The meeting was geared towards helping educators implement the characteristics of Jesuit education[28] in the schools. I was happy to be out of South Sudan after almost one year. It was a time for rest and recuperation after the hard work that I had been engaged in.

I was also happy to see the town of Juba for the first time. Juba had a semblance of a modern city. It was much more developed than Wau and Rumbek. I learned later that most of the developments I saw in Juba at that time began after the signing of the peace agreement in 2005.

Juba is situated on the bank of the White Nile. In the nineteenth century, a trading post and a Christian mission were located in the vicinity of Juba in a place called Gondokoro. Juba was the main southern garrison during the Anglo-Egyptian condominium rule of the Sudan (1898-1956). The region was

---

[28] The main aim of Jesuit education is to ensure full growth of the person which leads to action that is guided by the spirit and presence of Jesus Christ, the Son of God, the man for others. Action based on sound understanding and enlivened by reflection on their experience; urges students towards self-discipline, initiative, integrity and accuracy.

infested with malaria bearing mosquitos. Blackwater fever was also common in the region. Gondokoro was a base for the illustrious explorer and campaigner Sir Samuel Baker during his expeditions in the area from 1863 to 1865, and from 1871 to 1873.[29]

Juba was established as a small town by Greek traders who were supplying the British Army with various merchandise during the British campaign in the south of the Sudan. The native Bari people inhabited Juba and the Gondokoro area. The Bari had an excellent relationship with the Greek merchants. The Bari people continued to be the main ethnic group in the Juba area in 2013.

The Greeks contributed to the development of what can be seen today at the Juba Market. They built the Greek quarter and a small suburb which is now called Hai Jalaba. The Greek also built other remarkable buildings in the town during the early days of its establishment. The Anglo-Egyptian authorities had planned to join the southern part of the Sudan with northern Uganda because of the cultural resemblance of the two regions. That plan was frastrated in 1947 by an agreement at the Juba Conference which voted for the unification of northern and southern Sudan with Juba as the main town in the south.[30] Juba became the capital of South Sudan on 9 July 2011, when the country became independent from the Sudan.

The city of Juba has a river port, and it was the southern terminus of traffic along the Nile River. Before the first and second Sudanese civil wars, Juba was a transportation hub in

---

[29] Alan Moorehead, *The White Nile*, (New York: Harper Perennial, 2000), 60.

[30] Roland Werner, William Anderson, and Andrew Wheeler, *Day of Devastation, Day of Contentment: the History of the Sudanese Church Across 2000 Years*, 2nd ed. (Nairobi: Paulines Publications Africa, 2010), 277-79.

the south of Sudan, with highways connecting it to East and Central Africa. In addition, steamboats could move freely up and down the Nile from the river port at Juba. However, because of the two wars, Juba can hardly be called a transportation hub anymore. Most of the transport infrastructure was destroyed. The river harbor is currently not in use due to disrepair. At the time of my arrival there in 2013, the United Nations and the Government of South Sudan (GOSS) were repairing the roads and other infrastructure that were damaged during the first and second Sudanese civil wars. Juba has a functional International Airport which was being expanded when I arrived there in 2013.

In April 2005, a few months after the signing of the Comprehensive Peace Agreement that ended the second Sudanese civil war, Jonah Fisher reported the following for the BBC from Juba:

> "Juba is the largest and most developed town in southern Sudan but remains a collection of mud huts and half-derelict buildings. The electricity supply is intermittent, and hardly anyone has running water. Juba remained under government control throughout the 21-year civil war despite being surrounded on all sides by rebel forces. Tens of thousands of troops and countless tons of military hardware were flown in to reinforce this island of northern control from repeated rebel Sudan People's Liberation Movement (SPLM) offensives."[31]

---

[31] Jonah Fisher, "Southern Sudan's Frontline Town," BBC News Wednesday, 20 April 2005, 07:17 GMT 08:17 UK

Fisher continued his description of Juba in the following way:

> "When under the terms of a peace agreement signed in January, government troops eventually withdraw, it will become the capital and seat of the new SPLM-controlled southern administration. In the meantime, the much smaller Rumbek is serving as a temporary capital. The transfer of power in Juba from the government to the SPLM will not be easy. The communities who live in Juba are not natural supporters of the ethnic Dinka-dominated former rebels. During the civil war, local militia armed by Khartoum fought against their fellow southerners. Juba's governor and leader of the pro-government Mundari ethnic group militia Clement Wani, says that in clashes in the 1980s, rebels sexually abused women in his ethnic group and killed civilians. Against a backdrop of such bitterness, the SPLM has set up an office on Juba high street. […] Perhaps with ethnic sensitivities in mind, former Juba resident and SPLM secretary general James Wani Igga (a Bari) headed the first former rebel delegation. "After the fight, you are reconciled, and you become friends again," Mr. Wani Igga said from the comfort of the government guesthouse. "We are here for reconciliation and here for forgiveness.""[32]

There was no Jesuit house in Juba at the time of my arrival there. Previously, when the Jesuits taught at St. Paul's Seminary

---

[32] Jonah Fisher, "Southern Sudan's Frontline Town," BBC News Wednesday, 20 April 2005.

at Munuki, an outskirt of Juba, the Jesuits arriving in that city would be accommodated at the seminary. The only Jesuit who lived in Juba at that time of my arrival there was Fr. Michael Schultheis, SJ. He was resident at the Catholic University of South Sudan. He lived in a crammed apartment just enough for one person. I had to find a separate accommodation during my stay there.

I learned a lot about Jesuit education at the meeting in Nairobi. Most of the meeting time was devoted to exploring how the characteristics of Jesuit education could be implemented in the schools in the Eastern Africa Province. I also learned about *Cura Personalis* that individualized care of persons under my tutelage. That became a hallmark of my work with my students when I got back to Wau.

Chapter Ten

Travelling Mercies

"An evangelizing community is always concerned with fruit, because the Lord wants her to be fruitful. It cares for the grain and does not grumble or overreact."

Pope Francis (*Evangelii Gaudium* 24)

The treacherous, if not torturous road that runs between Wau and Rumbek is what Robert Frost would call "a road less travelled by." If only I had a choice I always wanted to avoid travelling along that road, yet the road kept beckoning me. I had to travel on that road again in June of 2013. The road hardened me up for the difficulties that were ahead in my mission!

In mid-June 2013, I travelled safely from Wau to Rumbek. It took us about ten hours in that 220 kilometers distance because the road was in very bad condition. I was scared to arrive in Rumbek at a late hour.

I took that opportunity to go to Rumbek so that I could check with Loreto Girl's Secondary School if we were on the right track with our implementation the new South Sudan syllabus. The Irish Loreto Sisters at Loreto Girl's Secondary School in Rumbek had implemented the new South Sudan syllabus in 2008, and they had had graduates for two years by 2013. Their experience was invaluable for us. I wanted to see how they were running the new curriculum and also borrow some of the materials which they had.

The Loreto Sisters in Rumbek were experts in the new South Sudanese curriculum, and so we were happy to learn from them. I was happy to realize that we at Loyola were on the right track. I was so inspired to see the young Loreto Sisters working with a lot of joy in that isolated situation. They were clearly motivated by the love of God as they worked with the young Dinka girls. They were giving those girls a valuable education that would change their lives. Dinka girls were disadvantaged because they were married off at a very early age and so most of them never went to school. The Loreto Sisters were attempting to break that vicious cycle. The Sisters were "women for others" whose love and care amazed me. They were open to collaborating with the Jesuits. They were clearly more engaged with the people wholeheartedly. Their motherly care for the Dinka girls moved me to reflect on how I cared for my students back in Wau.

* * *

Rumbek had experienced months of instability before my arrival there. Consequently, the new governor of the region had banned the sale of alcohol in the town. It looked like Sharia Law had been imposed on the town! Floggings were a common occurrence in Rumbek at that time. The governor banned alcohol in the town because he claimed that alcohol was the main cause of violence which was prevalent in Rumbek. Many people had been killed a few weeks before due to inter-clan wars. This was not true because the violence in Rumbek was connected to a revenge culture among the various clans coupled with a culture of cattle rustling.

One evening during that visit, I took a walk with one Jesuit around Rumbek. There, we met some disillusioned Ugandan motorbike riders who complained that their business opportunities had dwindled after the ban of alcohol which led to the closure of all bars in the town. Social life in Rumbek revolved around alcohol, and the ban affected most of the other businesses. These Ugandans were contemplating to return home because the government had also started banning foreigners from doing the motorbike transport business. They were saddened by all that was happening.

The ban on alcohol in Rumbek at that time was accompanied by random searches of households by the police who looked for any evidence of the presence of alcohol. Even if they found an empty bottle of alcohol that was enough evidence to land someone in trouble.

One day, as we were at breakfast, our Ugandan cook was hurriedly called to go to her house because an impromptu search was taking place in her area. Rumor spread around Rumbek that the ban did not affect the government officials, the SPLA, the police and the new governor himself. It was said that the 'big people' of Rumbek used to smuggle alcohol from lorries that were stopped at a checkpoint some miles before they got into Rumbek town on their way to Wau. Crates of alcohol were taken from those lorries and transported clandestinely to the 'big people' of Rumbek town.

* * *

During that visit to Rumbek, I met Fr. Richard O'Dwyer, SJ from the Irish Jesuit Province who was in the process of taking over from Fr. Francis Njuguna, SJ as the director of the Multi-Educational Agricultural Jesuit Institute of South Sudan (MAJIS) in the village of Akol Jal. Fr. O'Dwyer, a quantity surveyor, had worked with the Jesuit Refuge Service (JRS) in Sudan and South Sudan in the area of Lobone. He introduced many agricultural initiatives that made a positive impact in the farming practices in Lobone. It was hoped that he would help improve the farming situation in Rumbek through the MAJIS project. He described his endeavors in Lobone in the following way:

> "In January 2009, when I first arrived in Lobone, I was overwhelmed by the sheer beauty of its green fertile valley, surrounded as it is by densely forested mountains on three sides. These corners of Magwi County have plentiful rainfall and are dissected by fast flowing rivers, so even a city boy like me could see it had the potential to be an agricultural paradise. In my early days in Lobone, I discovered that comparatively little of the valley was cultivated. People spoke of their gardens rather than their farms, used hoes as the sole means of digging and cultivating the soil, and so I met subsistence farming for the first time in my life. Because cultivation was done entirely by hand the vast majority of the people cultivated a small garden of maize or sorghum, producing only enough food to feed themselves and their family."[33]

---

[33] Richard O'Dwyer. "An Experiment in Farmers' Education by JRS in Lobone" JRS Eastern Africa Newsletter. No. 50, July 2013.

Because of the above situation, Fr. O'Dwyer decided to introduce the ox plough, which was used widely in other parts of Africa, in Lobone. This changed farming activities in the area. The locals increased their farming capabilities to a great extent.

I found Fr. O'Dwyer to be a likeable man and it was nice to be with him. He had lots of interesting stories to tell. He took me to visit the farm in Akol Jal. I was shocked to see the many developments that had taken place there. There were many building in the farm which were not there six months earlier. A new mission had just begun from scratch! There was a classroom block with two classes, a staff room and a director's office. There was a residence for about four people and a huge storage facility. There were two water tanks connected to a borehole which had a solar pump. These water tanks could hold about 40,000 liters of water at once. The work done there was impressive considering the challenges involved in building infrastructure in South Sudan.

This was a fine example of a mission began from scratch with dedication and courage. I was impressed by Fr. Njuguna's efforts. He had no experience of working in such a difficult situation, but he made something beautiful out of it. Fr. O'Dwyer, who had more experience in building new missions, would bring his experience which would take Akol Jal to the next level. At that time, Fr. O'Dwyer was trying to raise the walls of the houses which had not been roofed in order to allow a good circulation of air in the houses. The modifications were necessary because of the high temperatures experienced in South Sudan.

Fr. O'Dwyer was joined in January 2014 by a Polish Jesuit, Fr. Tomasz Nogaj, SJ. Fr. Nogaj had an interest in hunting. Fr. Nogaj had written a book titled *Priesthood and Hunting*. After his arrival in Rumbek, he happened to chance upon a small baby antelope that had lost its trucks in the bushes near the farm in Akol Jal and was in danger of being eaten up. He took that baby antelope home and took care of it in his room in the Jesuit community in Rumbek!

In 2014 activities in the farming school expanded to include pastoral activities in the area. Fr. Nogaj reported the following from Akol Jal when the assistant of the Jesuit Superior General in Rome, Fr. Fratern Masawe, SJ visited the farm:

> "Since he (Fr. Masawe) was mostly interested about the faith and social dimensions of our work he was able to see the outcome of our pastoral work himself by attending a Eucharistic celebration at the farm. Since Holy Thursday 2014, as a result of having Masses every Sunday in Akol Jal and preaching the Gospel, we meet people from this area not only during weekdays, when we work in the farm, but also on Sundays for prayer services. During the Eucharist with Fr. Masawe, people were singing, dancing, clapping and even jumping. Fr. Masawe shared some stories from Rome with the participants in the Eucharist. He told them about Fr. General, and Pope Francis. There were about 60 people at the Mass in Akol Jal. A certain Elizabeth, who is a lay leader of the community, addressed Fr. Masawe at the end of Mass and asked if the Jesuits could help build a Catholic Church in Akol Jal. She said that such a church would help bring peace and stability in the troubled region."[34]

---

[34] Eastern Africa Jesuit News Update 14:26 June 27, 2014.

This was a mission that was promising to be a beacon of hope in a situation where it was easy to give up and get disillusioned. The situation was difficult, but the courage that the Jesuits showed was incredible. It encouraged me to trust in God and work hard for the greater glory of God.

* * *

I went back to Wau after five days in Rumbek. After straggling on the Wau-Rumbek road for hours, we entered Cueibet town in a snail's pace. Cueibet is a small village town with a few shops and few semi-permanent buildings. I felt relieved because we had finished the worst stretch of the road from Rumbek to Wau. We stopped at Cueibet to get some fresh air and relax.

Cueibet is home to the Dinka Gok clan which is hostile to the Dinka Agaar of Rumbek. Cattle raiding is a common occurrence in that area. This is the main reason why Cueibet and its environs is insecure. The Dinka Gok have been accused of raiding cattle in the Lakes region and other neighboring regions such as Warap.

In July 2013, the Jesuits of Eastern Africa were requested to take up the operation of a new teacher's training college for the Diocese of Rumbek which was being built in Cueibet. The college was situated close to the Cueibet-Tonj road. Some Comboni Missionary Sisters were living close to the compound of the proposed college. A group of South Korean missionary priests were also working in a new parish about 20 kilometers south of Cueibet in a place called Agangrial. These two religious groups have never experienced the violence first hand because the local people do not attack church facilities and church personnel unless they are provoked. The Cuiebet area is in need of evangelization and reconstruction. Later on, Br. Herbert Leibl, SJ said that the Jesuits could not simply say no to the work at the college at Cuiebet because it represented the preferential option for the poor.

The dream of a TTC in the Diocese of Rumbek was the brainchild of the late Bishop Caesar Mazzolari, MCCJ. He began thinking about it in 1990 when he became the Apostolic Administrator of DOR. He involved the Jesuits, with whom he enjoyed a cordial relationship, from the beginning.

At that time, in 1990, Father Mazzolari began developing a programme for basic education for all interested dioceses of the Sudan. In a letter to Fr. Paul Besanceney, SJ who was the Jesuit superior of Eastern Africa, Fr. Mazzolari wrote:

> "Briefly, the basic education programme, or "Bush School Programme" is aimed at developing a three-year elementary education plan to provide basic literacy, numeracy, general knowledge and fundamental agricultural and technical skills and knowledge of faith in general. This would equip the youth for social and economic survival and offer an essential step for eventual further education."[35]

In that letter, Fr. Mazzolari asked Fr. Besanceney if he could allow American Jesuit Fr. Edward Brady, SJ to be the director of the project. Fr. Brady was an experienced educator who had worked with the UN in the Sudan for many years. In 1990, Fr. Brady was in Khartoum, but he would eventually have to move

---

[35] Letter to Fr. Paul Besanceney, SJ on March 11, 1990 by Fr. Caesar Mazzolari, MCCJ, Apostolic Administrator or Diocese of Rumbek.

to Wau where Fr. Mazzolari was going to be stationed before he found ways of opening up pathways into his Rumbek territory.

Fr. Mazzolari continued in his letter:

> "There will be an interdiocesan central coordinating office in Khartoum, which I would like to see it being headed by Father Edward Brady, SJ with the cooperation of Father Philip Sina, who will be coming to Khartoum to stay. Father John Ashworth of the Mill Hill will also be part of this central office in Khartoum. [...] My specific request in this letter is to ask whether Father Richard Cherry, SJ who is stationed in Wau could lend a hand in supervising the shaping and furthering of the "Bush School Programme" for Wau and Rumbek among the youth in Wau." [36]

The "Bush School Programme" led to the development of a Christian Teachers Training Center (CTTC) which trained teachers who worked in the "Bush Schools" around Wau and Rumbek. The CTTC was inaugurated on August 27, 1990, by the then Fr. Rudolf Deng Majak, Apostolic Administrator of the Catholic Diocese of Wau. Three Bush Schools around Wau were used for experimentation purposes. The CTTC was based in Wau town, in the Mission compound opposite St. Mary's Cathedral, and was run jointly by the dioceses of Rumbek and Wau. Jesuit Fathers Cherry and Brady were actively involved in the CTTC during its time of inception and operation. The

---

[36] Letter to Fr. Paul Besanceney, SJ on March 11, 1990 by Fr. Caesar Mazzolari, MCCJ.

CTTC operated for two years and was closed because of logistical reasons.

* * *

After the closure of the Wau-Rumbek CTTC, the idea continued to mature in Bishop Mazzolari's mind. Eventually, when he had properly established the Diocese of Rumbek, the idea come up again. In 2010 with the help of funds from CESAR, a donor agency he helped to start, the building of the college commenced in the little market-town of Cueibet. Unfortunately, Bishop Mazzolari died in 2011 before the college was opened.

The college was expected to open its doors in February 2014, but the civil war that began in December 2013 in South Sudan made the opening to be impossible. On January 16, 2014, Fr. A. E Orobator, SJ wrote the following about the college in relation to the civil war that was ongoing in South Sudan at that time.

> "[…] the consensus is to move ahead with the discussion with the Diocese of Rumbek (DOR) in view of making a formal acceptance of DOR's offer. An oft-repeated phrase during the Province Assembly was "We need to go there!" Let me note that talking about another mission in South Sudan at a time of brewing conflict and uncertainty may sound counter-intuitive, at best, and foolhardy, at worst. Yet, if we are to believe our claims to be men of the frontiers, that is, where others would rather not go, a serious consideration of this

mission would seem a natural thing for us to do. But prudence counsels that we proceed cautiously. In anticipation of a favorable outcome of the peace talks, in the coming days, I will request DOR to develop an initial MOU, in view of seeking Father General's approval for the apostolic project."[37]

In November 2014, Jesuits established their presence at Cueibet as administrators and teachers in the new teacher's training college. It was named Mazzolari Teacher's Training College (MTTC) after Bishop Caesar Mazzolari.

Through my encounters and travels inside South Sudan, I continued to meet men and women totally dedicated to God's mission of proclaiming the Good News amidst despair. Meeting these people deepened my love for God's people in South Sudan, and also the meetings helped me to be attentive to God's presence even amidst the difficulties and challenges that I was experiencing as I lived in that volatile situation.

---

[37] Circular letter from Fr. A. E Orobator, SJ, superior of the Jesuits in Eastern Africa on January 16, 2014.

Chapter Eleven

Where God Weeps

"There is the Music of Heaven in all things and we have forgotten to hear it until we sing."

St. Hildegard of Bingen

If Sudanese politics was a bedeviled by racial identity between the Muslim Arabs and Black Christians that led to the two civil wars (1955-1972 and 1983-2005), South Sudanese politics has been marred by inter-ethnic tensions. There are more than sixty tribes in South Sudan. However, inter-ethnic tension is always high between the two main ethnic groups: the Dinka and the Nuer.

On December 6, 2013, a group of disgruntled senior members of the Sudan People's Liberation Movement (SPLM) led by Dr. Riak Machar Teny-Dhurgon, Ms. Rebecca Nyadeng Garang de Mabior, and Mr. Pagan Amum Okiech held a press conference in Juba. Dr. Machar was the Vice President of SPLM while Mr. Amum was the Secretary General. Both had been dramatically sacked from the Government of South Sudan (GOSS) in the summer of 2013 by President Salva Kiir Mayardit. Since the separation of South Sudan from the Sudan in July 2011, Dr. Machar had been the Vice President of South Sudan whereas Mr. Amum served as Minister for Peace.

After that press conference on December 6, it was decided that these disgruntled members of the SPLM would organize a rally to speak to the people about the bone of contention within the SPLM. That rally was scheduled for December 14, 2013. However, an SPLM meeting for the National Liberation Council (NLC) had also been arranged for the same day. Thus, the rally planned by the disgruntled SPLM members was called off in the spirit of solidarity with the mainstream SPLM. The disgruntled leaders of SPLM did not want to give an impression that they were opposed to the party by letting the rally take place at the same time as the NLC meeting.

Thus, on December 14, 2013, all the SPLM leaders including the disgruntled group attended the meeting for the NLC at Nyakuron in Juba. Present at the NLC conference were Archbishop Paulino Lukudu Loro, MCCJ the Catholic Archbishop of Juba, Archbishop Daniel Deng Bul of the Episcopal Church of the Sudan (ECS) and Ms. Hilde Frafjord Johnson the then head of the United Nations Mission in South Sudan (UNMISS). Archbishop Lukudu opened the conference with a word of prayer and a speech on reconciliation and dialogue among the SPLM members. All the religious leaders present were aware of the tensions that were looming within SPLM and the consequences of the tensions to the whole nation. Ms. Johnson spoke in the same line as Archbishop Lukudu, urging the different groups within SPLM to dialogue and reconcile.

As the first day of the NLC was underway, it became clear that the disgruntled members of the SPLM were ignored and even insulted. None of their grievances were addressed, and they were not given a chance to speak during the conference. Thus, the resentful members decided to boycott the meeting that was to continue the next day, December 15, 2013.

The absence of these members from that meeting was an opportunity for speculation among the ranks of the SPLM. Some argued that a coup was being organized by the absent members. This situation brought back memories of 1991 when Dr. Machar rebelled against the then leader of SPLM, the late Dr. John Garang de Mabior claiming that he was undemocratic.

* * *

In the evening of December 15, 2013, some soldiers in the Sudan People's Liberation Army (SPLA) headquarters in Juba were asked to surrender their weapons. It was feared that Dr. Machar had orchestrated a coup by inciting the soldiers loyal to him. Some soldiers at that barracks in Juba refused to be disarmed, and tension began to rise. Random gunfire was heard. The tension quickly evolved along ethnic lines with Dinka and Nuer soldiers pointing the finger at each other. A power struggle began to manifest itself with the Dinka soldiers supporting President Salva Kiir and the Nuer soldiers supporting Dr. Machar. The Nuer and the Dinka are the majority in the SPLA and, thus, this tension was potentially explosive.

The Dinka Nuer hostility runs back in time. The history, culture, and mythology of these two ethnic communities reflect this antagonism. The two communities are cattle keepers and since they live side by side, cattle raiding is common among them, and this is accompanied by killings on both side. Each person killed had to be avenged even after many generations. This vicious cycle runs deep.

* * *

On the night of December 15, 2013, as skirmishes were erupting at the Juba garrison, word started to spread that a coup attempt was in progress and tension was high in the country and beyond. Many expatriates began to leave the country. As things were unfolding President Kiir went on the television, in full army regalia, and announced that there had been an insurrection at a garrison in Juba and it had been contained. In that televised address, he mentioned Dr. Machar's 1991 defection from the SPLM/A. The army regalia that the president was wearing pointed to something more serious than what he was saying. His body language left a lot to be desired. Things seemed to be falling apart. Were we on the brink of a third civil war in South Sudan?

In the following days, after the appearance of the President on television, things seemed to spiral out of control. The whereabouts of Dr. Machar was unknown. It was said that initially, he had fled to the UN compound in Juba and then he later disappeared into the bush. Many people were killed in Juba in the first few days of the hostilities.

Some leaders of the SPLA who were advocating for reforms were arrested in Juba on the pretext that they were planning a coup. They remained under arrest even after pressure from the international community that they be released. These group remained in detention for many weeks. Speaking to the *London Evening Post*, Ms. Garang said that the accusation about a coup attempt planned by those advocating for reforms within the SPLM was a fabricated propaganda.[38]

During the first few days of the tensions, fierce fighting emerged in the town of Bor, the capital town of the volatile Jonglei region of South Sudan. It was said at that time that Dr. Machar was organizing his rebel army from there. Bor is about 200 kilometers from Juba, and it was feared that the rebels would march into Juba and take over the government. Many soldiers were sent to Bor to stop the rebels from advancing. In the process, many civilians died. International media showed bodies lying on the streets of Bor.

* * *

The Kenyan government began evacuating its nationals who were mainly business people in Juba and many other towns in South Sudan. A US military helicopter was brought down by the rebels in Bor while on a mission to evacuate US nationals from there. Four marines were injured. Three Indian UN peace keepers were killed at the UN mission at Akobo.

The fighting quickly spread across the oil producing regions of Jonglei, Unity and Upper Nile. The towns of Bentiu and Malakal became scenes of war for many weeks. Both towns were taken over by the Nuer led rebels several times within the first months of the war. Bitter fighting between the government forces and the rebels led to the loss of many lives.

The Apostolic Administrator of Malakal Diocese, Monsignor Roko Taban Mousa, had to leave the diocese for

---

[38] Exclusive interview with Rebecca Nyadeng on the situation in South Sudan. January 25, 2014. http://www.thelondoneveningpost.com/exclusive-rebecca-nyandeng-garang-reveals-all-how-salva-kiirs-private-army-prompted-the-current-conflict/.

many months because of the war that was taking place there. He was hosted by the Diocese of Wau. John Ashworth wrote the following about what was taking place in Malakal:

> "In the town of Malakal in Upper Nile State, for example, Catholic Bishop Emeritus Vincent Mojwok protected civilians in his house during two rebel takeovers. On the third attack, however, he was persuaded to leave as it became clear that the rebels were no longer respecting churches as places of refuge and were deliberately targeting the Shilluk ethnic group. The elderly bishop waded up to his neck in the River Nile as bullets splashed into the water around him, and then walked for days through the bush before reaching safety. He has lived through two previous civil wars but says he has never seen anything like this before. His colleague and veteran peace-builder Bishop Emeritus Paride Taban sadly observed that South Sudan has become the place where God weeps."[39]

As the hostilities continued, it was feared that the planting season would find people away from their farms and, thus, no crops would be planted. This would then lead to a famine situation. That seemed to have been the case because the civil war continued into the planting season in Bentiu, Malakal and other northern towns.

Fr. Salvador Ferrão, SJ was in his occasional itinerant missions in Maper and Alor areas, during Christmastime 2013.

---

[39] John Ashworth. "South Sudan: Peace is Possible."
http://thinkafricapress.com/south-sudan/peace-possible-kiir-machar.

He had been trying to evangelize those isolated areas of the Diocese of Rumbek for many years during Christmas and Easter. He wrote the following entry in his journal about the experiences he had there at that time:

> "It was Sunday 22 December 2013, I travelled to Alor-Maper Mission, over 100 kilometers north of Rumbek. In the early hours of Tuesday, a truck brought extra soldiers to the sixth division. They were blowing horns calling on youngsters to get ready to be conscripted and be ready to launch attacks on the rebel soldiers of the deposed Vice President Dr. Riak Machar. The opposing armies confronted each other in running battles in the nearby payams (districts). Instead of singing "joy to the world" they brought wounded colleagues back to their base. I went to anoint them. One soldier "conquered the heavenly battle" after receiving the holy oils of Christmas. Late on Christmas Eve, again horns were blown and gunfire was in the air. "A silent night a holy night certainly not, but a bloody night." We prayed the rosary in front of a new cross which had just been erected. We asked for forgiveness for the war that was going on. Meanwhile, the wounded soldiers were being transported to the local dispensary. I gave the wounded biscuits, tea and soap as well as Christmas blessings. On Christmas morning, no one had come for Mass. As I went back to the house I remembered

what the late Bishop Caesar Mazzolari, MCCJ told me years ago, 'Do not get kidnapped again.'"[40]

As the violence was taking place in other parts of the coutry, the town of Wau remained peaceful, although tension was high in the town. Everyone was alert, anything could happen at any time.

* * *

By the first week of January 2014, the situation in most towns in South Sudan had normalized with the exception of Bor, Bentiu, Malakal and Maban which are all in Jonglei, Unity and Upper Nile regions. Some alarmists in international media, social media and in private communication claimed that the war affected all parts of the country and that it was getting worse by the day. This was not true.

I came to learn, from my lived experience in South Sudan, that war situations usually appear worse to the outsider than to the people living in those situations. The Jesuits continued with their ministries in Juba, Wau and Rumbek trusting that God was in charge of the situation. Those Jesuits who were out of the country returned in January to join their companions in the saving work of God. On January 6, 2014, Fr. A. E Orobator, SJ the Jesuit superior of Eastern Africa; wrote the following about the situation:

> "As a province, we will do all that we can to continue to bear witness to the love, reconciliation,

---

[40] Journal entry by Fr. Salvador Ferrão, SJ on December 27, 2013.

justice and peace of the risen Christ by our mission and ministry in South Sudan. All the Jesuits who are currently in South Sudan are staying on and carrying on with their mission and apostolates. They deserve our prayer, support and encouragement. We encourage all our friends and well wishers of South Sudan, wherever they may be, to do all they can to advocate on behalf of South Sudan for a speedy, just and peaceful resolution of the current crisis. In particular, we call on the international community not to abandon South Sudan; to ensure that adequate provision is made for the security and protection of innocent civilians, especially women and children; that there is sufficient humanitarian assistance for refugees and internally displaced people; and that appropriate pressure be exerted on the principals to the conflict to cease hostilities and resolve their differences through dialogue and peaceful political means."[41]

* * *

On January 18, 2014, I travelled back to South Sudan from my Christmas break in Kenya. On that day, as I was disembarking at the Juba International Airport (JIA), I saw a huge Russian Antonov plane parked close to where I was disembarking together with other passengers. Many people were carrying domestic paraphernalia such as mattresses, blankets, pots, and

---

[41] Circular Letter No. 153 of 6 January 2014, On the Situation in South Sudan and our Companions in the Country by Fr. A. E. Orobator, SJ Jesuit superior of Eastern Africa to the Jesuits in the Province.

pans, etc., and were running to board the Antonov. I later learned that those were people from north Sudan who were being given a free ride back home because of the tense situation in South Sudan. I also saw many people seated at the airport's waiting area stranded with their belongings. They looked so desperate. There were many military people guarding the airport. I saw some Ugandan helicopters and soldiers on standby. The UN soldiers with their blue helmets could also be seen patrolling the airport.

Watching what was unfolding that day at JIA made me feel so sad. These people had suffered decades of war, and now the only chance for peace was about to be taken away. I felt so helpless. I wanted to do something to help the situation, but there is nothing I could do. I just surrendered the situation to God. I was so afraid because of the number of soldiers wielding their M-16s who were standing there looked trigger happy. I thought that shooting could start at any time. However, deep within me, I could feel God's abiding presence with me guaranteeing that all will be well and that I was not to lose hope.

The number of displaced people three weeks after the war began was enormous. The Jesuit Refugee Service (JRS) was overwhelmed by what was happening. JRS personnel had to be evacuated several times out of the Maban area which is near Malakal town because of the fighting that went on for months on end. The same happened to the workers of the other NGOs working in the area to alleviate famine and provide other basic necessities to the people.

* * *

When I arrived in the city of Juba in January 2014, I found that life had gone back to normal although there were many military people stationed around the city. All the military people who were strategically placed around the city, had new black machine guns (M-16s). There were several UNMISS patrol cars that were moving around. Some SPLA trucks full of soldiers were also seen speeding up and down in the streets of Juba.

On my first night in Juba, there was sound of automatic gunfire close to the place I was staying. We were quickly told not to worry because those were the National Security people who were a little tipsy and were trying to scare the hell out of the people who did not obey the 6:00 p.m to 6:00 a.m curfew who were still moving around the city. I stayed in Juba for three days before getting a flight to Wau. The town was at peace although there was a lot of tension. A curfew had been enforced in the city, and most of the businesses closed early.

After the outbreak of civil war in December 2013, all commercial flights inside South Sudan were suspended except the government owned South Supreme Airlines. The company doubled the price because of the huge demand for travel that was created by the suspension of the other flights. The suspension of the flights was motivated by the fear that privately owned planes could be used by the rebels to transport firearms. The United Nations Humanitarian Air Service (UNHAS) flights continued to be available, but it was increasingly difficult to get a seat in those planes.

It was hard for me to get a flight to Wau on my return to Juba in January 2014. Thus, I spent three days waiting for the next available plane. As I waited in Juba for a flight to Wau amidst the turmoil, I kept reminding myself that as a witness to the Gospel message of Christ, I am called to stand with

God's people. I saw many NGO people being evacuated at Juba International Airport. I felt so scared and unsure if I should be getting into the country or getting out like what the NGO people were doing. However, I reminded myself that I am not an NGO personnel, but a person motivated by a Christ-centered mission that urges me to stay with the people who are suffering and oppressed when they need consolation, support, and reassurance. That thought made my return to Wau easy; I felt confirmed by God that I was doing the right thing.

* * *

From January 21 to 31 2014, the Sudan Catholic Bishop's Conference (SCBC) met in an Extraordinary Plenary Assembly in Juba. The Bishops of the two countries (Sudan and South Sudan) continued to belong to one episcopal conference even after the separation that occurred in 2011.

The SCBC bishops went to Juba in January 2014 to reflect on the situation of the country and to pray for the restoration of peace and stability. After a ten-day meeting, they produced a pastoral exhortation titled "Let Us Refound Our Nation on a New Covenant." In it, the bishops proposed solutions to the crisis that the country faced and also offered a message of hope to the people. Part of the pastoral exhortation read as follows:

"This crisis has been caused by many issues which need to be addressed:

> (a) We have witnessed the growing tensions within the governing party, the SPLM. The failure to deal with these through internal party mechanisms has played a significant role in the escalation of tension

that preceded the violence that erupted on 15th December 2013. Democratic reform is urgently required within the SPLM. Internal party disputes should not be allowed to destabilize the nation. (b) We stress the need for better governance. Too often we see the tendency to personalize political power, to behave in ways counter to the best interests of our communities, a failure to appreciate that public office is a service to the people. Our institutions across the country need to be staffed by individuals chosen for their competency and professionalism. (c) Corruption and nepotism have contributed to the destabilization of South Sudan. This has prevented basic services from reaching the people and is breeding resentment and disillusionment towards the institutions of our state. (d) Our history is an open wound that desperately needs healing. We must heal our society by allowing our communities to tell their stories openly and without fear. Negative narratives fester and poison our social relations. We retell them in our villages to our children. Let us end these vicious cycles by creating space where we can speak and work towards peaceful coexistence and reconciliation." [42]

Although a cease-fire between the government and the rebels had been signed in Addis Ababa, Ethiopia on January 23, 2014; fighting continued unabated in Upper Nile, Unity and Jonglei

---

[42] Sudan and South Sudan Catholic Bishops Conference (SCBC). "Let Us Refound Our Nation on a New Covenant." Pastoral Exhortation after a meeting held in Juba from 21st-31st January 2014.

regions. The leader of the rebels in Malakal publicly stated that he was not going to abide by the cessation of hostilities agreement that had been signed in Addis Ababa. Later on, both the rebel and the government sides claimed that they were forced to sign the agreement by the Ethiopian Prime Minister, Hailemariam Desalegn, or face war crime charges in The Hague. Several other agreements were signed in Addis in 2014, but the war continued.

Bishop Emeritus of Diocese of Torit (DOT), Paride Taban and the Episcopal Church of Sudan (ECS) Archbishop Daniel Deng Bul participated in the peace process, but their call for peace was not heard by the opposing sides. Bishop Taban had been working for peace and reconciliation in South Sudan for many years. He helped begin the Holy Trinity Peace Village in Kuron village which is in Narus Parish (DOT) in which diverse people live in peace.

Comboni Missionary Sr. Elena Balatti, CMS wrote the following account as she was preparing to evacuate from Malakal in the end of January 2014:

> "On Wednesday, the 26th, a group of people from Christ the King Church rushed to the UNMISS. Even old women with sticks pushed themselves ahead on the long and dusty road. In the night, the rebel soldiers had taken away nine girls. A few had come back in the morning after having been raped. One of them was 12 years old. There was no longer any kind of security even at Christ the King church. Malakal had become virtually an empty town, void of civilians. Even domestic animals could no longer be seen. Vultures and dogs were feeding on the

corpses. Groups of rebels were the only ones moving around. The last images I had from Malakal while heading to the UNMISS aircraft bound to Juba were the corpse of a woman who appeared to have been raped and the smoke of the villages set on fire on the Western bank of the Nile. A comment made by many people was re-echoing: How can they say that they want to come to govern us if they are killing us and destroying everything?"[43]

The UN High Commissioner for Human Rights Navanethem Pillay visited South Sudan at the end of April 2014. She met both President Salva Kiir and Dr. Riak Machar in Juba and Nasir respectively. She urged them to reconcile and help stop the civil war. Her plea seemed to have fallen on deaf ears because the civil war continued unabated. The two leaders could not agree. In a Press Conference in Juba Dr. Pillay said the following:

> "The deadly mix of recrimination, hate speech, and revenge killings that has developed relentlessly over the past four and a half months seems to be reaching boiling point, and I have been increasingly concerned that neither South Sudan's political leaders nor the international community at large seem to perceive quite how dangerous the situation is. Unfortunately, virtually everything I have seen or heard on this mission has reinforced the view that the country's leaders, instead of seizing their chance

---

[43] See Chronicle written by Comboni Missionary Sister, Elena Balatti, CMS. http://combonisouthsudan.org/.

to steer their impoverished and war-battered young nation to stability and greater prosperity, have instead embarked on a personal power struggle that has brought their people to the verge of catastrophe."[44]

The two leaders were not ready to initiate change at that time. Dr. Pillay ended her speech in Juba in a rather helpless tone: "How much worse does it have to get, before those who can bring this conflict to an end, especially President Kiir and Dr. Machar, decide to do so?"[45] I felt so conflicted hearing those words of Dr. Pillay; I questioned God, "Why did you let all this happen?" God did not answer me that day.

* * *

The town of Wau continued to experience peace in the months of January through May 2014. The Jesuits of Wau were fortunate to continue with their school ministry without any interference. The same applied to Rumbek. Apart from the usual inter-clan fighting that was common in Rumbek, the Jesuits there continued with their work in peace.

To fully implement a new school curriculum in a place like Wau took a long time. Even when on the surface things looked all right, there was always something that needed to be fixed. That is the uncertainty that one had to endure with hope. A new

---

[44] Navarethem Pillay. "South Sudan on Verge of Catastrophe." Opening remarks at a press conference in South Sudan, Juba, 30 April 2014.
http://www.ohchr.org/EN/NewsEvents/Pages/DisplayNews.aspx?NewsID=14550&LangID=E.

[45] Pillay. "South Sudan on Verge of Catastrophe."

school year began at Loyola Secondary School in February 2014. We finally were successful in implementing the three terms system and moved away from the old semester system. With the three-term system, we had completed the implementation of the new South Sudan Curriculum at the school. I was happy to be part of that process; I was able to learn a lot from that experience.

At the same time, we got the whole school fenced thanks to donations from well-wishers. Because of the insecure situation in which we were living, we were happy that we could at least guarantee the safety of the school community. After the fencing was done, we realised that the school land which was previously cultivated by the local people from the community around the school could not be left to lie idle. We decided to start an agricultural project that would help the school raise funds for feeding our students.

* * *

The many Jesuits and other heroic people I met in South Sudan, some of whom I have recounted their stories in this narrative, inspired me to be close to the poor. I met one inspiring person who worked in South Sudan in an extraordinary way! I come across the journals of an iconic Jesuit who worked for many years in Sudan: Fr. Paul Besanceney, SJ. It was titled: *Sudan: An Occasional Diary*. This was a very special time for me, I felt revitalised in my work in South Sudan by reading the heroic work of service that Fr. Besanceney and the other pioneering Jesuits did in the Sudan. The journals were about five hundred handwritten pages.

The journal entries began in July 1980 when Fr. Besanceney

arrived in Juba and ended in Khartoum in 2004. Before coming to Sudan, Fr. Besanceney had served as a professor of Sociology at John Carrol University in University Heights, Ohio from 1963-1971. He became the superior of the Detroit Province of the Society of Jesus from 1971-1977. Then from 1977-1980, he moved to Washington, DC where he worked as an Assistant Researcher in Sociology at the Centre for Applied Research in the Apostolate (CARA) at Georgetown University, before coming to Sudan in July 1980. His time at CARA was a form of preparation for him to come to Sudan. He had a gift of leadership which would be very valuable during his time in Sudan and Eastern Africa in general.

Two years after his arrival in Sudan (1982), he was appointed rector of St. Paul's Major Seminary which was at Bussere in Wau. In the beginning, both theology and philosophy studies were being offered at Bussere and so Fr. Besanceney was, in essence, a rector of two seminaries. He later began a process of separating the seminaries, and he oversaw the process of building of the seminary in Juba at a place called Munuki. In 1985, the theology section of St. Paul's Major Seminary, Bussere was moved to Munuki, Juba. Fr. Besanceney continued to be rector of both the seminaries. He would stay for one semester in one seminary and the next semester in the other.

Fr. Besanceney arrived in Sudan three years before the second Sudanese civil war began. His journals read, in some parts, like a wartime diary. It is full of stories about the war. In 1986, Fr. Besanceney spent 108 days on the road as he was attempting to get to the philosophy section of St. Paul's Major Seminary at Bussere during the second semester. This was because the activities of the SPLA could not allow free movement and, thus, people had to travel carefully. At that time, it was usually safe to travel in a convoy which was protected by the military. On Thursday, November 27, 1986, at 6:00 p.m., he wrote the following in the diary after those 108 days on the road to Wau:

> "We spent two more nights south of the Bo River and one just north of it. Four lorries were able to cross the bridge, the next one fell in. The driver was not hurt much and the lorry and goods were pulled out later. Almost all of the men spent the next day either cutting trees to try to repair the bridge or carrying rocks to the part of the river where the water level was too high to be crossed. The second of these projects proved to be successful. Nearly a third of the lorries crossed over that evening. I was one of the first to drive across in the morning with Frs. Jervas and Enzo as passengers. The Land Rover went right across and up the rocky bank on the other side, in four wheel drive, without a sputter in spite of the fact that the water was flowing over our front fenders in a fast current. There was much excitement and many cheers at the end as hundreds were watching." [46]

Fr. Besanceney continued about the story of that eventful journey to Wau in the following way:

---

[46] Paul Besanceney. *Sudan: An Occassional Diary* (1980-2004), November 27, 1986.

"The soldiers from Wau had come to meet us at the river, and one of their tanks stood ready to pull us up on the other side with a cable if we got stuck. The lorry just before us had to be helped in this way because it could not get up the steep bank on the other side. Our next night after all had crossed was spent within a few miles of the river. Then we had a night in Baziia, where all lorries were parked in three columns close together, with a tank at each end, half expecting to be attacked that night by the SPLA. There had been two attacks there in the previous week so that local people had closed all their shops and withdrawn. As an exercise, the soldiers in the evening deployed themselves by fours a hundred feet from the perimeter of the huddled lorries. Our Land Rover was toward the front left side, outside the three columns of lorries. After eight days and seven nights on the road from Tombura, we arrived in Bussere about 3:00 p.m., tired but relieved. For me it was 108 days since I first tried to get from Nairobi to Wau (Bussere). The convoy was not allowed to go to Wau but they stayed overnight in Bussere to allow stragglers to arrive. On Tuesday or Wednesday another convoy arrived in Wau from Awiel. A third is waiting in Raga for an escort."[47]

In 1986, Fr. Besanceney oversaw the transfer of the philosophy section to Juba. The premises at Bussere were abandoned because the war had intensified, and this made Bussere inaccessible. The SPLA soldiers vandalized part of the

---

[47] Besanceney. *Sudan: An Occassional Diary.*

seminary after the move to Juba took place. In 2012, when I visited the seminary, it looked like a ghost town.

Fr. Besanceney continued to be rector of the seminary until 1988 when he was appointed superior of the recently created Eastern Africa Province. He served in that capacity for six years (1988-1995). He returned to St. Paul's Major Seminary, in 1995, where he served as Academic Dean from 1995-1999 and as rector from 1999 to 2003. St. Paul's Major Seminary had been transferred to Khartoum because of the war intensified in Juba in 1991. Fr. Besanceney continued teaching in the seminary until 2008 when he retired. During his time in the Sudan, he was an advisor to the Sudan Catholic Bishops Conference (SCBC). His journals reveal the extensive knowledge he had about the Sudan. He travelled widely within the Sudan, sometimes in merchandise lorries.

After he retired in 2008, he spent his time at Loyola House, Nairobi, Kenya; the headquarters of the Jesuits of Eastern Africa. He went back to Detroit in 2009 where he died at Colombiere Centre in Clarkston, Michigan. He was loved by many Sudanese clergy who knew him. His life gives me hope and courage to serve the people as a Jesuit "for the greater glory of God."

Chapter Twelve

Giving a Lifetime?

"You cannot be serious about the struggle of our people here unless you play and celebrate and do the things that make it possible to give a lifetime to it."

Anonymous Salvadorian Woman to an American Aid Worker

I enjoyed my work as a teacher at Loyola Secondary School, Wau. Even though the social situation was precarious, I felt God's presence and love guiding me. It was a time to depend on God's providence and love. Many times, I felt abandoned and insecure, but thinking about the local people who had no choice but to live in that situation, kept me going. I felt, as time went by that I had developed a deep love for the people and wanted to journey with them all my life. Living out of my comfort zone helped me grow in my trust in God's providence. When I felt insecure, I kept remembering that I was in God's mission and if I lost my life in the process, I would be received by God because I had said yes to God's call to spread the Good News.

The most exciting aspect of my experience at Loyola was that I was involved in the personal lives of the students. If I may use Jesuit language, I offered *Cura Personalis* to them.

Cura Personalis, in the Jesuit tradition of education, involves individualized attention to the needs of the other, distinct respect for his or her unique circumstances and concerns, and an appropriate appreciation for his or her particular gifts and insights. To the students that I was teaching, I made this my priority. I made an effort to understand them better. I was available to them all the times they needed me. I made it a habit to sit outside the classes during break times so that I could engage them in informal conversations. I was surprised by how open they were to me. I also developed a pedagogy of teaching them some moral lessons by use of stories which was very effective.

On my departure from South Sudan, Loyola Secondary School continued to grow amidst manifold challenges. The civil war that was ongoing at the time worried many people about the future of the school. It was hoped that the war would not spread to Wau. Even though the war was continuing in other parts of the country studies continued normally at Loyola. The students continued to take their studies seriously. Their smiles and laughter was a clear demonstration that they were full of hope. Their future was not going to be bleak.

Lack of enough qualified teachers is perhaps one of the major setbacks for the school. Implementing the new South Sudan curriculum, with English as a medium of instruction, continued to be a challenge for South Sudan because the few teachers available were trained in the old syllabus developed in Khartoum, north Sudan. This Khartoum syllabus was conducted in Arabic. Loyola has been a model school around Wau and South Sudan in the implementation of the new South Sudan school curriculum even though it has been an uphill task.

In the 1980s, the school accepted boys only as students. This was because culturally, girls were not allowed to venture out of their homesteads. This was a culture that treated women as servants of men. In 2008 the Jesuits made the school coeducational because of the increasing need of educating the girl-child in the South of Sudan. The school, at this point, is trying to educate future women leaders of South Sudan. It is helping to change a patriarchal mentality that women do not need to be educated because they are only fit to do menial tasks at home.

Loyola Secondary School continues to be a beacon of hope for the South Sudanese people despite its troubled past and the present challenges. Its students are promising, and the Jesuits hope that they will help to shape the future of the new nation. The parents are proud to have their children in the school. They appreciate the kind of valuable education that the Jesuits try to inculcate in their children.

My experience at Loyola Secondary School and the stories that surrounded it were and still are a consolation to me. I was happy to be part of a mission that directly touches "the fundamental option for the poor" in a radical and meaningful way. The overall experience was by no means easy, it was challenging, difficult and at times exhausting. It was a period of discovery which I cherish. Although it was a challenging experience, I was able to "seek and find God" in it. I had very many graceful and positive experiences that will define my life forever. Being able to make a difference in the lives of the people I ministered to made me feel consoled. Sharing my life with people who have endured one of the most horrendous historical injustices and being able to be a witness to them in a way that improved their own lives made me feel happy. I was doing what God wanted me to do at that moment.

God taught me from both the good and difficult experiences that I encountered. I learned to trust in the slow work of God. Many times I wanted things to be different, but I had to patiently wait as God worked God's ways. The experience taught me that I should always be ready to learn new things and adapt. I slowly developed a magnanimous spirit towards the difficult situations that I faced.

I did not imagine that I would write about my experiences and that of others in South Sudan when I first arrived there. Everything seemed new and overwhelming for me. It took me time to adapt to the new situation I was called to live in. I was eventually moved by the spirit of God to put down these experiences, and I hope they will be able to give hope and courage to those who will one day have the privilege to work and live amongst the people of South Sudan. The writing of this story kept changing as time went by. Stories kept coming to me as a re-membered my Jesuit journey in South Sudan. The stories of other Jesuits who went before me were collected from anecdotes that I was told and from written sources such and letters and diaries.

I was privileged to have had a chance to be part of the history of the Jesuits who worked in South Sudan. I am also proud to have taken part in the history of the people of South Sudan. Their history has become my story too and, in this chronicle, I narrate part of that story that I inherited by sharing in their joys and sufferings.

* * *

In my journey in South Sudan, I met men and women dedicated to the service of the people in great need. Their lives and enthusiasm for the saving work of God gave me a lot of encouragement and hope for the new country. I met many men and women who left their comfort zones in order to be with the poor people who needed their presence. Sometimes it was only that presence that was needed.

The enormous needs of South Sudan cannot be accomplished overnight. The presence of people who are in solidarity with the South Sudanese is what is more important. Witness to the Gospel values through a positive presence in the midst of misery is what Christ continually calls each Christian to do. Christian friendship and hospitality are the most important gift that the people of South Sudan need. The people of South Sudan exude humanity full of dignity and warmth. These people welcome you as a stranger who must become a friend.

I sat on a patio overlooking Juba University on my last day before exiting South Sudan reminiscing on what I had experienced. I was full of hope for the newly born country and its people. "God will not let down these people," I thought. Around that time, I happened to chance upon the words of Edward Hoagland in *African Calliope: A Journey to the Sudan*, about a particular evening he had in Juba which mirrored what I experienced that evening. I quote Hoagland's words below:

> "I should have been reading the Koran, but instead I browsed in the Bible for a familiar or soothing voice hearing, nevertheless, a Sudanese clamor in the Gospel according to Mark. Muslim prayers are more ritualistic and the Koranic God more distant than His Christian counterpart: God is seldom petitioned or pleaded with as through the intercession of Jesus, a Mary or a church pastor. But Juba is not Koranic,

and the events in Galilee, Judea and Jerusalem seemed much more plausible in Juba than they would in present-day Jerusalem or Europe's Christendom. Here, if they happened again, it seemed to me that they would be attended, and possibly accepted, with the same pitch of fervency. A healing, miracle–working savior who would be locked in a cage within an hour if he appeared in Los Angeles or London could resurrect himself in Juba and see the populace catch fire, believe the evidence of their eyes and make the sand streets resound again." [48]

Hoagland continued:

"Maybe for all this to happen, it is necessary that there be lepers sitting beside the road, lazy high-honed biblical kite, a blind albino girl with stumps for arms, a man bustling about on all fours with his thin buttocks canted as high as a baboon's because of a spinal injury that had never been treated when he was a child, and a hunter arriving on foot, carrying gazelle meat on a shoulder frame, with five spears in his hands, a brown bush hat, mud smeared on his neck and forehead to ward away the flies, and a calabash full of milk hanging from a thong around his neck. Another man stumped along on a eucalyptus stick strapped with a strip of goat hide to his left hip, followed by his wife with an enormous

---

[48] Edward Hoagland, *African Calliope: A Journey to the Sudan* (New York, NY: Lyons Press, 1978), 164-65.

fold of flesh which had gradually swallowed one ear and now was enveloping the whole side of her head. Miracles that would not happen in New York or Jerusalem might occur in a place where the Son of God, if he were arrested, might still be killed, not entrusted to the care of social workers and psychologists."[49]

Jesus is alive in South Sudan! Those who know how to see take off their shoes and recognize that they are standing on sacred ground. Through the difficulties, struggles and disappointments that the South Sudanese people experience daily, glimpses of the risen Christ who brings hope can be seen. The story I narrate in this chronicle describes my attempt to see Christ in people who live in a situation that can elicit despair rather than hope. Love for the people I served guided me to offer selfless service. With God, I was able to be "more" for the people of South Sudan and Wau in particular. Everything was accomplished in the presence of God, supported by private and communal prayer. My prayer as I end this story is: "God continue to bless the work of our hands."

* * *

The efforts that the Jesuits have made and are still making in their quest to help in the reconstruction of South Sudan is great. The Jesuits who have offered their lives to work in that "frontier" continue to inspire more young people to join the Society of Jesus in South Sudan. The lives of these Jesuits continue to inspire me to work for the "preferential option for

---

[49] Hoagland, *African Calliope*, 164-65.

the poor." The grain of wheat that has been planted in that fertile soil of South Sudan by the holy boldness of the Jesuits continues to sprout albeit slowly.

There is still more that needs to be done in South Sudan by the Jesuits. St. Ignatius of Loyola, the founder of the Jesuits, calls for *magis* or "more." The Jesuits in South Sudan need to "go further still." This is because the country is in great need.

According to my lived experience in South Sudan, education seems to be the greatest need for the country. Education is key in transforming a post-conflict situation such as South Sudan. Gordon Brown, the former British Prime Minister, observes that:

> "Education […] has a wider role to play. Armed conflict and the threat of violence remains a source of insecurity for many of South Sudan's people. Many factors are involved, including prejudice, long-standing hostilities, and attitudes that see recourse to violence as legitimate. With the right curriculum in place, the education system could act as a powerful force for peacebuilding, the development of shared identity, and the creation of a society that is more resilient and less vulnerable to violence."[50]

Brown continues to observe that:

> "The newly-independent country of South Sudan is anchored to the bottom of the world league table for

---

[50] Gordon Brown, *Education in South Sudan: Investing in a Better Future* (London: The Office of Gordon and Sarah Brown, 2012), 8.

education. More than half of its primary school age children – over 1 million in total – are out of school. Young girls are more likely to die in pregnancy or childbirth than to graduate from primary school. South Sudan's young people face restricted opportunities for the education they need to build a better future for themselves and their country. It is time for the world to come together and change this picture. […]."[51]

The two Sudanese civil wars (1955-1972 and 1983-2005) destroyed the education system in the south. Thus, the education situation there is dire. The need for creating more educational opportunities for the people in South Sudan is crucial.

The Jesuits are continuing to serve this need through the educational institutions currently in operation in South Sudan. The Jesuits are trying to deliver to the South Sudanese people what Gordon Brown calls the "education peace dividend."[52] Education seems to be the only road to the development and lasting peace in South Sudan. This endeavor is fraught with enormous challenges, some of which have been described in this story. I was privileged and happy to have contributed in delivering education peace dividend to the South Sudanese people. God was always on my side reassuring, challenging, and filling me with joy as I journeyed with God's people there.

---

[51] Brown, *Education in South Sudan*, 10.

[52] Brown, *Education in South Sudan*, 15

www.ingramcontent.com/pod-product-compliance
Lightning Source LLC
Chambersburg PA
CBHW022359040426
42450CB00005B/252